FAITH

&

WORK:

DO THEY MIX?

Os Hillman

ASLAN GROUP
PUBLISHING

Unless otherwise stated, Scripture taken from the *Holy Bible, New International Version*
Copyright © 1978, 1984 by International Bible Society. Used by permission of Zondervan Publishing
House. All rights reserved.
The "NIV" and "New International Bible" trademarks are registered in the United States Patent
and Trademark Office by International Bible Society.
Use of either trademark requires the permission of International Bible Society.
Scripture quotations marked KJV are from the King James Version.
Scripture quotations marked RSV are from the Revised Standard Version, copyright ©1952, Division of
Christian Education of the National Council of Churches of Christ in the United States of America.

Printed in the United States of America
ISBN 189306594-4

Aslan Group Publishing
3595 Webb Bridge Road
Alpharetta, GA 30005-4140
770-442-1500

Table of Contents

Acknowledgements

I wish to express special thanks to my editing team: Charis Hillman, my daughter; and Billy Burke, my long-distance editor in Japan. Special thanks to Angie, my wife and editor who always gives valuable feedback to my work. Thanks also to Merriana Brannan for assisting with the layout and design.

Bless you all for your valuable input and direction on this project.

Dedication

To Gunnar and Aster Olson, who have demonstrated what it means
to walk with Jesus in the marketplace in love, humility, grace and power.
Thank you for mentoring so many of us around the world.

My message and my preaching were not with wise and persuasive words,
but with a demonstration of the Spirit's power, so that your faith might not rest on men's
wisdom, but on God's power (1 Cor. 2:3-5).

Introduction

Faith and work: Do they mix? Every Monday morning millions of people around the world go to work forgetting what they did on Sunday and move across an imaginary demarcation line. This says there is little relationship between what they experience on Sunday and what they do on Monday. Or, is this really the case? Perhaps I am making an assumption that is incorrect. Are there statistics that can tell us any different? Does our culture reflect any evidence to the contrary?

For years those of us in the Christian faith have heard terms like "full time Christian work" or "I am called to the mission field" or "I'm in the ministry" and any number of terms that are designed to designate a distinction between one who is working "full time" versus one who is a "layman". The inference is that the layman "works" for money whereas the minister "works" for God.

There are two questions we hope to answer in this book. First, does faith and work really mix in the Monday through Friday, nine to five world of most people? Second, does God make a distinction between the "full time" Christian worker and the layman"? Is there a heavenly class distinction between these groups? Does one person have greater spiritual marks for being "full time" compared to one who is "part time"?

I must confess right up front that I believe the answer to the question raised by the title of this book, *Faith and Work: Do They Mix?* has a convincing answer of "Yes, faith and work do mix and they should mix!" We will help you see for yourself from scripture why this is true and why you as a Christian cannot live a segmented life that views work and faith as two different worlds. If you do, it is doubtful you are experiencing God in a way that He wants you to experience Him, nor are you having a satisfying work life. After all, Christ's nature never changed based on the environment where He lived. He experienced the divine nature of God whether he was mingling with tax collectors, speaking to the Pharisees, or preaching in the synagogue. He performed miracles wherever He was—at a wedding, at a home, or in the marketplace. It was the need and the situation that determined His response.

Therefore, let's find out why some believe faith and work don't mix, and why I believe they do.

1

Sacred Versus Secular

*The LORD God took the man and put him in the Garden of Eden
to work it and take care of it (Gen. 2:15).*

Imagine for a moment that Jesus has just completed his three years of training with the disciples. He has been crucified and is now commissioning the twelve to go into the world and disciple the nations. Now imagine him also making this statement to them.

> *"Dear brothers, it is now time for you to share what you have learned from me. However, as you share with others be sure that you keep what I taught you separate from your work life. The principles I have shared with you only apply in situations outside your work life. Do not make them fit into this context. The miracles you saw in me can only be done in certain situations outside your work life. Keep this in mind when thinking about praying for the sick or the lost. These truths will not work in the marketplace."*

Sound preposterous? It may, but this is the mindset of many in our world today. The spiritual does not mix with the everyday world of the workplace. "What happens on Monday has no relationship to what takes place on Sunday," they say. These are the thoughts expressed so much in our day and time, although they are not expressed in such direct terms. Let's think more about this idea. When Jesus came to earth, how did He come? As a carpenter. A man given to work with his hands and to provide an honest service to his fellow man. He did not come as a priest, although He was both a King and a Priest (Rev. 1:6KJV). When it came time to recruit those for whom the church would be founded, He chose twelve men from the marketplace—a fisherman, a tax collector, a doctor, and so on. They all came from the marketplace. Interestingly enough, none of his disciples were priests in the Jewish church, a natural place to recruit from if you were going to start a religious movement. Jesus called them all from the marketplace of life. Was this any accident that Jesus called men and women from the marketplace to play such a vital role in His mission? I think not.

When God created the earth, He demonstrated something right up front to human beings. He believed in work. He was above all else, the Master Creator. He was an artist, designer, strategic planner, organizer, project developer, assessor, zoologist, biologist, chemist, linguist, programmer, materials specialist, engineer, and waste management technician. This work did not end when He created man, but was only the beginning in His continued care for mankind. Whether we call our work "sacred" or "secular", all legitimate work reflects the activity of God. God is honored when we work with the goal of reflecting His life through our life and work. So why and how did society begin to draw a separation between faith and work?

The Great Divide: Elevating the Spiritual at the Expense of the Secular

If you were to conduct a survey on an average city street to determine if people thought religion belonged in the workplace, chances are high that they would say no. Most people today see no relevance between God and work in today's fast-paced marketplace. Why is this? Why do many Christians even believe this? Well, it goes back to our early years.

Os Guinness, in his book, *The Call,* provides us the necessary history of how we got to this segmented view of work and life.

> The truth of calling means that for followers of Christ, everyone, everywhere, and in everything lives the whole of life as a response to God's call. Yet, this holistic character of calling has often been distorted to become a form of dualism that elevates the spiritual at the expense of the secular. This distortion may be called the "Catholic Distortion" because it rose in the Catholic era and is the majority position in the Catholic tradition. Protestants, however, cannot afford to be smug. For one thing, countless Protestants have succumbed to the Catholic Distortion as Wilberforce nearly did. Ponder for example, the fallacy of the contemporary Protestant term "full-time Christian service"—as if those not working for churches or Christian organizations are only part-time in the service of Christ. For another thing, Protestant confusion about calling has led to a "Protestant Distortion" that is even worse. This is a form of dualism in a secular direction that not only elevates the secular at the expense of the spiritual, but also cuts it off from the spiritual altogether.[1]

---

[1] Os Guinness, *The Call,* p.32., Word Publishing, 1998, Nashville, TN.

Therefore, it is understandable why we are where we are today. Over many centuries, we have been trained to believe that the two worlds of spiritual and secular are to be separated. Now it is easier to understand why the separation of church and state is such a debated issue.

"Full time" vs. "Part time"

May the favor of the Lord our God rest upon us: establish the work of our hands for us--yes, establish the work of our hands (Ps 90:17).

Throughout the church, a view of those in full-time Christian work versus those who work "secular" jobs has created a definite class distinction. There seems to be little evidence of this distinction in the Bible. Yet, we often hear testimonies from those who left "regular" jobs to go into the mission field, or some other "full-time" Christian work.

My good friend, Rich Marshall, has been a pastor for more than thirty years. He came into this understanding of the walls that existed between sacred and secular. He came to recognize the calling that men and women had to the workplace, so he began ordaining men and women in his congregation for their call to the workplace. Rich came to realize that so often his fellow ministers had been guilty of training those in the marketplace to do the church's ministry instead of their ministry. And these are not necessarily the same, nor do they require the same skills. In his book, *God@Work*, Rich writes the following regarding two words (clergy and laity) that have brought confusion to the true call of men and women to the marketplace.

Two little words, words that misrepresent God and His plan, have been used by the enemy to bring about the development of a caste system within the Body of Christ—those who are called to "professional ministry" or "full-time ministry" the "clergy"; and those who are not: the "laity." It is my conviction that all of us in the Body of Christ are called to "full-time" ministry. When we allow this caste system to disturb our thinking, we create a problem for many who experience the strong call of God on their lives. We need both a terminology and a mindset that works to eliminate the "second-class citizen" concept in the Kingdom of God.

John Beckett is a business leader who has written an excellent book for business leaders: *Loving Monday*. In it he tells of his own journey into understanding the call of God. He writes, "For years, I thought my involvement in business was a second class endeavor—necessary to put bread on the table, but somehow less noble than the more sacred pursuits, like being a minister or a missionary. The clear impression was that to truly serve God, one must leave business and go into 'full-time Christian service.' I have met countless other business people who feel the same way."[2]

The often-held view by pastors toward business people was brought home to me one day when I received a letter from a pastor in response to an internet devotional that I write for men and women in the workplace. This devotional is being distributed throughout the world and I have a surprisingly large number of pastors subscribed to it. One day I received a very simple note from a pastor that said, "How can a businessman have such wisdom?" This comment spoke volumes to me. Basically, he was implying that clergy were the only ones in tune with the spiritual matters of life, and businessmen and women are focused on the "secular" life. However, God has never said this. He is now helping many of us begin to understand our true calling as disciples of the Lord Jesus, but with different roles to fulfill in the body of Christ. And no role is less Holy than another.

When I received Christ in 1974, I was a golf professional. God gradually led me away from golf and into business. In 1980, I considered moving into "full-time" Christian work by attending a short-term Bible school to determine if I wanted to be a pastor. I served briefly as an assistant pastor only to have the position removed. God took me out of that because it was never His intention for me to be a pastor.

It was more implied guilt than a genuine call of God that led me to consider "vocational ministry". I believed I might not have been giving my all to God if I wasn't full time in the work of the Lord. I have learned since then that work truly is worship to God: work and worship actually come from the same root Hebrew word, avodah. If you are in a secular job that doesn't violate scripture, your vocation is just as important to God as is a full-time missionary in India. God calls each of us to our vocation. It is in that vocation where He desires to use us for His kingdom.

In their book, *Your Work Matters To God,* authors Doug Sherman and William Hendricks state the following regarding holy versus unholy vocations.

The architect who designs buildings to the glory of God, who works with integrity, diligence, fairness, and excellence, who treats his wife with the love Christ has for the Church, who raises his children in Godly wisdom and instruction, who

---

[2] Rich Marshall, *God@Work,* p.5, Destiny Image Publishers, Shippensburg, PA June, 2000.

urges non-Christian coworkers and associates to heed the gospel message -- in short, who acts as a responsible manager in the various arenas God has entrusted him -- this man will receive eternal praise from God. That is what really matters in eternity. In short, God's interest is not simply that we do holy activities but that we become holy people. Not pious. Not sanctimonious. Not otherworldly. But pure, healthy, and Christlike.

This whole idea of secular versus religious is a Greek idea. These Greek ideas, clothed in biblical language, have for the most part, been passed down unchallenged to succeeding generations of Christians. As a result, most of us today bring assumptions to the biblical text, assumptions based on a workview articulated by Plato, Aristotle, Plotinus, and other Greek thinkers. Likewise, if you have been around much Christian teaching, you've undoubtedly been influenced by at least some Greek ideas. Nothing overtly or purely pagan. But I suggest that Christianity in our culture has absorbed from its tradition a number of subtle beliefs that trace back to Greek philosophy. Now I am not 'down' on philosophy. Nor am I 'down' on the Greek philosophers, for they have provided us with many insights into philosophical questions. Nevertheless, reading the Bible through their eyes -- through Greek glasses -- can severely distort the truth of God's Word. We will think that the Bible says things it does not say, and overlook important things it does say. The result will be a distorted view of life. And a distorted view of work. Wearing Greek glasses, one would tend to ignore or disparage everyday work. This is how work looks when viewed through these lenses.[3]

Sherman makes an excellent assessment here of how many Western societies have been affected by the philosophies and culture of the Greek influence. We in the United States may speak English, but we think "Greek". Our focus on competition, segmentation of life from the secular to sacred, rationalism and reasoning—all move us to a goal of a more intellectual position in our faith instead of a simple trusting faith. The root of this is the Greek/Hellenistic civilization. It has been so much a part of our thinking and way of viewing life that we have lost our ability to understand God and relate to him as the early church did.

---

[3] Doug Sherman and William Hendricks, *Your Work Matters To God* (Colorado Springs: NavPress, 1987), 60.

As the church grew and extended its borders outside Jerusalem believers became influenced by a wide array of philosophies. The purity and power of the message were affected by the dominant culture, which became the Greek culture. The time following the two major Jewish revolts of AD 70 and AD 135 saw a Greek, man-centered view of the world reshape the church. Early Greek scholars like Plato introduced dualism, which says that life is divided into two compartments: the spiritual or eternal, and the temporal realm of the physical. Plato's dualism entered the church through many of the church fathers that were Greek philosophers who had converted to Christianity. They attempted to reconcile Greek thought with Christianity.

To Bring Glory to God

God takes us through the process of life and allows us to develop specific skills and talents for His purposes. The marketplace is where many of us have the greatest opportunity to display these gifts. When young David went up against Goliath, he was only a small shepherd boy. King Saul offered David his armor to protect him from the big Philistine, but David knew the weight of the armor would be a hindrance to him. Instead, David used the skills he had developed as a shepherd to protect his sheep. A slingshot and stones were his weapons. When the time came for David to exercise his faith in God to slay the giant, he used the talents God had trained him to use. The shepherd fields were David's training grounds. There he learned to fight lions and protect his sheep. Now he would protect God's sheep. God gives us the same talents to achieve the things He wants us to achieve. However, not all of us will be heroes. Some of us have been called to use our talents to serve others to benefit the kingdom of God. David's faith was the reason God gave him victory. David declared that he came in the name of the living God and that the whole world would know the God of Israel because of the defeat of Goliath by a small shepherd boy. This is why God gave him victory over Goliath -- so the world may know the living God. The workplace is a training ground for most of us. It is the place where we deal with the everyday challenges of life, but it is also here where God wants to reveal His glory "so that the world might know that He is God." Someone once said that you will have many "jobs" before you come into the "primary" calling God has for your life. I have seen this principle at work. God uses the early training, like David, to prepare us for future battles and future experiences that God will use for his purposes in our lives.

That is how God wants to use you and me, so we may proclaim Him wherever we are. He also wants us to use the talents and abilities he has allowed us to be trained with for His greater glory in this world. For many of us, these talents were given to provide valuable services to our employers for the glory of God. We can find comfort in the knowledge that there is no higher calling than to be where God calls us regardless of whether it is in "full-time" Christian mission work, or working at the local hardware store.

Our Primary Call

We should step back for a moment and remind ourselves again that each of us is called to a personal relationship with God through Jesus Christ, first and foremost. From this position all else comes. The fruit of our relationship with Christ moves us to the level of our calling in work. That work—whether serving on the mission field or delivering mail -- is a holy calling of God. The reason God holds a high view of work is that He created each person in His image for an express purpose in this world to reflect His glory in ALL aspects of life. *And whatever you do, whether in word or deed, do it all in the name of the Lord Jesus, giving thanks to God the Father through him* (Col 3:17).

He knows the number of hairs on our head, and He knows what we are wired to do in life (see Ps 139). By segmenting this part of our life, we cut off the expression of His life to the world. However, He would by no means let us do that. He knows there are many who will never hear the gospel because they will never enter a church building. You or I may be the only representative of God they will ever encounter.

Have you ever considered the diversity of gifts and talents God gave humankind? It is amazing to consider. I sometimes think about someone who is working in a particular profession that does not appeal to me, yet God created that person to use his or her gifts for that express purpose. At the same time, He desires that we see work as worship to Him and a place where His presence and power can be manifested as a testimony to the world. God is always about creating a testimony of His love and power for the world to see. The Bible is a continual testimony about reconciling the world unto Himself. Later we will see how God has demonstrated His life through individuals in some dramatic ways in the workplace.

The Value of Secular Work

The *Word in Life Study Bible* provides some good insights into this question of secular versus sacred work.

God values our work even when the product has no eternal value. Christians often measure the significance of a job by its perceived value from the eternal perspective. Will the work last? Will it "really count" for eternity? The implication is that God approves of work for eternity, but places little value on work for the here and now. By this measure, the work of ministers and missionaries has eternal value because it deals with people's spiritual, eternal needs. By contrast, the work of a salesman, teller, or typist has only limited value, because it meets only earthly needs. In other words, this kind of work doesn't really "count" in God's eyes. But this way of thinking overlooks several important truths.

(1) God himself has created a world that is time-bound and temporary (2 Peter.3:10,11). Yet he values his work, declaring it to be "very good," by its very nature (Gen 1:31; Acts 14:17).

(2) God promises rewards to people in everyday jobs, based on their attitude and conduct (Eph 68; Col 3:23-4:1).

(3) God cares about the everyday needs of people as well as their spiritual needs. He cares whether people have food, clothing, and shelter.

(4) God cares about people who will enter eternity. To the extent that a job serves the needs of people, God values it, because he values people.[4]

Skillful Work

Do you see a man skilled in his work? He will serve before kings; he will not serve before obscure men (Prov. 22:29).

The Lord has called each of us to be excellent in what we do. Those whom God used in the Kingdom as marketplace ministers were skilled and exemplified excellence in their field. Not only were these men skilled, they were filled with God's Spirit. (Then the Lord said to Moses,) *"See, I have chosen Bezalel son of Uri, the son of Hur, of the tribe of Judah, and I have filled him with the Spirit of God, with skill, ability and knowledge in all kinds of crafts-to make artistic designs for work in gold, silver and bronze, to cut and set stones, to work in wood, and to engage in all kinds of craftsmanship"* (Exodus 31:1-5).

---

[4] *Word in Life Study Bible notes*, p. 1869, Thomas Nelson Publishers, Nashville, 1993.

Consider Huram, the master craftsman of bronze to whom Solomon entrusted much of the temple designs. He was a true master craftsman (see 1 Kings 7:14). Consider Joseph, whose skill as an administrator was known throughout Egypt and the world. Consider Daniel, who served his king with great skill and integrity. The list could go on—David, Nehemiah, Acquilla and Priscilla. Most of these were in the "secular" world of work providing a service that was needed for mankind. May we strive for excellence in all that we do for the Master of the universe. *Whatever you do, work at it with all your heart, as working for the Lord, not for men, since you know that you will receive an inheritance from the Lord as a reward. It is the Lord Christ you are serving* (Colossians 3:23-24 emphasis mine).

Reflection

1. What has been your personal experience of the concept of "sacred" versus "secular?"

2. Have you ever considered your job a ministry? Explain.

3. Based on the information in this chapter, explain why God views secular work as important.

CHAPTER 2

My Journey

In order to give you a perspective on how I came to investigate this entire area of work and faith it is important for you to understand a little of my own journey.

I was raised in an upper middle class family in the South. I was the only boy among five children. My dad was a successful businessman in the toy industry. He began his career owning and operating a toy store, and was probably one of the first pioneers to use television to sell products in the late 1950s. His program was thirty minutes long, and featured many of the new toys during the Christmas season. He would direct people to the store. Today, we call these infomercials. During the late sixties, my dad's business sold more than 2 million yo-yos, an impressive number for this period. During that same time they introduced a great selling toy called The "Slinky", which had actually been a little known airplane part before it made its debut. Dad was a great businessman.

While I was growing up, I was very active in sports and my dad was a great encourager in this area. When I was eleven I began to play golf and became a very good junior player. By the time I was fourteen years old, I had broken 70 three times< and by sixteen I had had three hole-in-ones. However, when I was fourteen my dad was killed in an airplane crash. Our family had always been a church-going family, but we knew little of the concept of walking in a personal relationship with God. This accident ultimately led my Mom to a more intimate relationship with God. Over the next several years, my goals were focused on playing golf for a living. I received a golf scholarship to the University of South Carolina. When I finished school I turned pro only to become frustrated with my inability to get to a level to play competitively as a professional. This frustration would ultimately lead me to finding my purpose in life beyond golf, which was now only becoming a wearisome and empty life. Finally, through the influence of my mom and a pastor, I became a Christian in 1974.

As the years went by I decided that golf was no longer the profession I felt God wanted me to be in. I made a career change into the workplace to sales and marketing. After being in various careers for six years I ultimately found myself longing to grow more in the Lord and serve Him more. I was involved in starting a church with two other men who were seeking to be used of God. This led me to begin thinking about whether I was "really sold out" for God and whether I needed to go to seminary. "Perhaps I was really called to be a pastor," I thought to myself. I decided to take a leave of absence from my job and go to a three month Bible study course held in California. This school was associated with churches all over the United States and made the students aware of the needs of local churches throughout the country. I decided to move to Atlanta to serve as an assistant pastor only to have the position removed after three months. This led me back to the business world and in hindsight, I see that it was the hand of God. I ultimately learned that I was never cut out to be a pastor or in a "vocational ministry". I was designed to be in business. On the other hand, I could not help but think of myself as a "second-class" Christian who was not quite sold out to the purposes of God. I don't know that anyone was saying this to me, but it was more implied by the culture.

For the next fourteen years I would invest my life in business as a Christian seeking to reflect Christ in my work. I began an ad agency in 1984, and was able to serve many high profile clients like American Express, Steinway Pianos, Peachtree Software, and many national Christian organizations. Our work received many international marketing awards. I felt I was a pretty good Christian business person who gave more than ten percent of my income to the church, shared my faith with others, and showed myself as a model Christian among my peers. At the same time there was another side to myself that was not totally evident to me at the time. I struggled with my marriage relationship and discovered that I had an increasing focus on building financial security.

In 1994, my world fell apart. I had made enough money to retire if I had wanted to at the age of 44. I was playing golf about three times a week. I had a life that many would have longed for. My walk with God was "adequate" in my eyes and did not see that I was much different from any other Christian businessperson I knew. Then one day my wife of fourteen years announced she wanted to separate. This would lead to a divorce three years later. Investments of more than $500,000 disintegrated over a period of a few months. Also, 80% of my business was lost during the same period along with clients who failed to pay bills that added up to more than $140,000. My world quickly changed from having a successful small business and family, to having no family, little money and a shell of a business. I was devastated.

I recall having heard stories of other business people in the past that had gone through difficult times. I always looked at them with a judgmental attitude thinking they made unwise choices and reaped from those choices. My problems, though, did not stem from unwise choices. At least they didn't appear that way to me. I was forced to find answers. I was in enough pain that I needed to find answers. So, for the next two years I would seek answers. I questioned what I had done wrong and why God had allowed this to happen to me. The first year a man came into my life who would provide one piece of the puzzle. He helped me to work on control issues related to my character. The next year another man would come into my life that would provide insights into what God was trying to accomplish in my life. Finally, two years into the process I was sent an audio tape from a Swedish business man named Gunnar Olson. He was the founder of the International Christian Chamber of Commerce. In that tape he talked about a phenomenon going on in the world he called the "Joseph Process". He described how many people went through great trials in their business life as part of a calling by God to be a Joseph in their day. This peaked my interest a great deal, and when I learned Gunnar Olson was going to be in Washington, D.C. in a month to host their international conference, I knew I needed to go and meet him.

The year leading up to this meeting was a year in which I had begun studying the scriptures to find out what God said about adversity, faith and work. I had begun studying the life of Esau, who despised his birthright and bartered it for porridge. It was interesting to compare the life of Esau to those in the workplace who did not understand their true calling to the workplace. I studied the life of Joseph and how God used the adversity to lead him to an ultimate calling in his life, but through much testing and trials. During this time, I launched a magazine called *Christians In Business,* only to have it die after one issue due to lack of funding. That would be yet another lesson in this pilgrimage of learning to walk with God in the workplace amidst great trials. By the time I flew to Washington to meet Gunnar I had more than three hundred pages of material written on the subject.

When I walked into the suite with Gunnar and fellow board member James Lockett, I was invited to sit down. Gunnar asked me to tell my story. For the next few minutes I recounted my narrative in every gory detail. When I finished, he looked at James and began to chuckle. At that moment I did not know whether to stand up and leave or smack the guy. I could not believe his response. He immediately apologized and said, "We are not trying to be rude to you, we have simply heard this story so often that it is uncanny to us. Be assured, my friend, you are one of God's Josephs that He has called." At that moment life began to take on a whole new perspective. For the next few minutes Gunnar pulled out a napkin and began to draw two diagrams that became the centerpiece of understanding for me regarding what I was going through.

As I returned home the next day I realized that the two years leading up to this encounter were not merely two bad years, but preparation for something God had in mind for my life, even though I had made mistakes that I was deeply sorrowful over. An encounter I had just thirty days earlier now made sense to me. Some of the pieces of this strange puzzle were now beginning to form a picture. I mentioned earlier that God had brought a man into my life who discipled me in areas where I had never been trained. I was discovering many new spiritual truths about myself and other Christians in the workplace. I came to identify with the struggles of Esau and Joseph in their desire to understand their own birthrights. I began to write about these discoveries to help other businesspeople understand their own callings through business. One morning on a weekend getaway in the mountains, my friend looked at me and said, "Do you know the meaning of Omar?" My full real name is Omar Smallwood Hillman III. Dr. Smallwood had delivered my grandfather, but no one, not even my mother, knew the origin of "Omar." They put the "O" and the "S" together to call me "Os." "You need to know the meaning of 'Omar'," said my friend. "It has something to do with your future." Startled by his assertion, I looked up the name of "Omar" that night on a computer program. Here is what I found: "Arabic for first son and disciple, Hebrew for gifted speaker, and German for famous. Rooted in the Middle East, this name is rarely used in the West. Omar was the great grandson of Esau." I was shocked. I had just completed 300 pages of material on the relationship of Christian businessmen to the life of Esau. My friend quickly concluded that God had called me to free Christian businessmen and women from the "Esau life". It was God who had allowed me to receive a name that related to the person of Esau. It was the closest thing to a burning bush experience I'd ever had. Could the Lord be this personal with us? *These were the chiefs among Esau's descendants" The sons of Elphaz the firstborn of Esau: Chiefs Teman, Omar, Zepho, Kenaz* (Genesis 36:15).

A Genuine Movement

A few months later I had lunch with Larry Burkett, the president of a ministry called Christian Financial Concepts. Larry had written a great deal about Christian business practices and had created a workshop called *Business by the Book* that had been developed many years earlier. I met with Larry to share with him my observations about what seemed to be an extraordinary trend of new grassroots marketplace ministry groups being born throughout the country. He was not aware of the trend but asked if I might invite some of the major marketplace ministries to a roundtable discussion for the purpose of comparing notes. I agreed and invited the top four or five ministries that I was aware of to a roundtable discussion. I sent a fax invitation to the heads of these groups and they, to my surprise, agreed to meet. As the days went by, I began to get requests from others to whom I had not sent invitations asking if they could attend this meeting. By the time the meeting was held, more than fifty-five leaders showed up representing forty-five different organizations throughout the U.S. Then, to my shock, Larry Burkett had to cancel due to a conflict in his schedule. I was left to host the meeting by myself. It was at this meeting where we learned that God was doing something new among those in the workplace, and that He was allowing ministries to be raised up to serve those who work there. This became the birth of Marketplace Leaders, an organization designed to help raise up men and women to understand their rightful calling to the workplace. Since that 1997 meeting, God has taken me out of the country several times and has confirmed this call upon my life. He has connected me with leaders within this movement throughout the world. I have seen this movement grow at an alarming pace and can say first-hand that God is raising up an army for His purposes in these last days.

It is from this backdrop that I speak to you through this book. Since 1944, I have been on a fast track of understanding the Biblical calling of men and women in the workplace, and watching the move of God bring this area into focus. There is a genuine movement taking place, and there is a specific reason God is doing this.

Reflection

1. In my personal story, why do you think the adversity was necessary for God to bring me into the calling He has for my life?

2. Based on the information in this chapter, do you believe there is a worldwide movement taking place in the workplace?

3. Why do you think God is doing this at this time in history?

3

The Rise of Spirituality in the Workplace

"Spirituality in the workplace is exploding."
    --Laura Nash, Harvard Divinity School and author of *Believers in Business*

Every Monday morning Janice travels across town in Southfield, Michigan, to attend a Bible study for businessmen and women. At one time, there were only a few who met in the office of Dr. Victor Eagan's orthodontic practice. Now, they have had to move because more than fifty people show up each Monday at 6:30 in the morning.

Today, the study is on conflict in personal relationships. People around the room share how God has helped them deal with difficult relationships. Some even shed a tear as they tell how difficult some relationships have been, but they confide that God wants forgiveness among Christians towards each other. It's just another Monday in Janice's life, but she admits it's the most important day of the week. "This is where I hear practical advice of incorporating my faith into my career. Church is great, but here I learn how to practically implement the Bible in everyday life," she comments. "There is a hunger among men and women in business to know what God says about their work," says Dr. Victor Eagan, President of Workplace Wisdom Ministries. "They are realizing that their calling in life is their work, not the mission field of Africa. More and more people are desiring to know how to practically implement their faith with their work."

Is there really a move of God in the workplace today?

The story above is repeated throughout the country as men and women are realizing that making the buck is not the only criteria for a successful life. Even the secular media is recognizing that something is going on. Articles on faith in the workplace have appeared the last two years in *USA Today, Businessweek, U.S. News & World Report, Harvard Business Report, and Christian Science Monitor,* to name just a few. No longer are people turned off with the idea of the importance of mixing faith and work.

An article in the November 1999 issue of *Business Week* magazine titled *Religion in the Workplace* cites:

> A spiritual revival is sweeping across Corporate America as executives of all stripes are mixing mysticism into their management, importing into office corridors the lessons usually doled out in churches, temples, and mosques. It is no longer taboo to talk about God at work.

> Across the country, major-league executives are meeting for prayer breakfasts and spiritual conferences. In Minneapolis, 150 business chiefs lunch monthly at a private, ivy-draped club to hear chief executives such as Medtronic Inc.'s William George and Carlson Co.'s Marilyn Carlson Nelson draw business solutions from the Bible. In Silicon Valley, a group of high-powered, high-tech Hindus—including Suhas Patil, founder of Cirrus Logic, Desh Deshpande, founder of Cascade Communications, and Krishan Kalra, founder of BioGenex—are part of a movement to connect technology to spirituality. In Boston, heavy hitters such as retired Raytheon Chairman and CEO Thomas L. Phillips meet at an invitation-only prayer breakfast called First Tuesday, an ecumenical affair lang shrouded in secrecy. More publicly, Aetna International Chairman Michael A. Stephen has extolled the benefits of meditation and talked with Aetna employees about using spirituality in their careers.

> That's not to mention the 10,000 Bible and prayer groups in workplaces that meet regularly, according to the Fellowship for Companies for Christ International. Just five years ago, there was only one conference on spirituality and the workplace; now there are about 30. Academic endorsement is growing, too: The University of Denver, the University of New Haven, and Minnesota's University of St. Thomas have opened research centers dedicated to the subject. The number of related books hitting the store shelves each year has quadrupled since 1990, to 79 last year. The latest: the Dalai Lama's *Ethics for the New Millennium*, a new business best seller. Says Laura Nash, a business ethicist at Harvard Divinity School and author of *Believers in Business*: "Spirituality in the workplace is exploding".

In part, what's happening is a reflection of broader trends. People are working the equivalent of over a month more each year than they did a decade ago. No surprise, then, that the workplace—and not churches or town squares—is where American social phenomena are showing up first. The office is where more and more people eat, exercise, date, drop their kids, and even, at architecture firm Gould Evans Goodman Associates in Kansas City, Mo., nap in company-sponsored tents. Plus, the influx of immigrants into the workplace has raised awareness about the vast array of religious belief. All over the country, for example, a growing number of Muslims, such as Milwaukee lawyer Othman Atta, are rolling out their prayer rugs right in the office.

With more people becoming open about their spirituality—95% of Americans say they believe in God or a universal spirit, and 48% say they talked about their religious faith at work that day, according to the Gallup Organization—it would make sense that, along with their briefcases and laptops, people would start bringing their faith to work.[5]

What we see from this article is not only is there is an openness to Christianity in the marketplace, but there is also a broader movement to embrace all forms of spirituality. This should be a concern for Christians.

Ten years ago, one could only identify about 25 formal organizations that existed to help business people integrate their faith with their work. Organizations like Christian Businessmen's Committee (CBMC), Full Gospel Businessmen Fellowship International, and Fellowship of Companies for Christ (FCCI) were typical. Today, well over 900 organizations that have a national or international focus have been formally identified.

Henry Blackaby, author of the best-selling *Experiencing God* Bible study series was asked where God was moving the most today. In February 2000, he cited the workplace as one of the major areas. "I see two areas. I"m hearing a heart-cry from the CEOs in the business world. I recently began having a monthly CEO conference call with two men. Just two days ago, we spoke to over 40 in four separate groups, an hour at a time, men from all kinds of Christian faith backgrounds. There is an avalanche of CEOs from major companies—the 'movers and shakers' across the nation who have heard about this and want to be involved. They want to know, 'How do I

[5] *Businessweek* magazine, Nov 1999, *Religion in the Workplace.*

relate my relationship to God as a Christian CEO to the workplace?' When we talk with them about the fact that, in the Bible, most all of the activity of God that changed society was done in the workplace and not in the church, suddenly the lights come on and they say, "How can I then make decisions in the workplace that make a radical difference?"[6]

This movement has seen more and more Christian enterprises birthing to serve the growing need to service those in the workplace who desire to integrate faith and work. Many of these have begun within the last five years. Workplace Wisdom Interactive is one of the new breeds of "marketplace ministries" seeking to help men and women incorporate Biblical faith with their work through a unique website designed to "bring the wisdom of God into the workplace" by placing hundreds of articles on a website for free access (wowi.net). It was founded by Dr. Victor Eagan and his wife Catherine. Dr. Eagan is an orthodontist by trade and has a practice that is in the top 2% in the world. His wife is a graduate of Harvard who came from a banking background and rose to the top in her profession. Today, God is using this couple around the world to speak into the lives of men and women in the workplace.

Life@Work Journal, a publication that was begun in 1998, is a quality magazine addressing the needs of men and women in the workplace and experiencing rapid growth with successful distribution through Barnes and Noble bookstores, Christian bookstores, and a growing list of subscribers (lifeatwork.com).

Bob Buford, a successful cable television executive came to realize how little impact his life was having on his culture as a businessman. He needed to see his life count more for spiritual causes and decided to do something about it. He wrote a book called *Halftime,* in which he shares his own journey to find meaning and purpose from his work. He realized that he wanted to spend the second half of his life to impact the world he lived in. So, he founded FaithWorks, an organization that encourages men and women to use their gifts to impact the social sector of society (faithworks.org).

Fellowship of Companies for Christ International (FCCI) is a ministry devoted to helping Christians who own businesses use their business as a platform for ministry. The ministry began in 1984 and has a worldwide membership of Christian CEOs (fcci.org).

Nehemiah Partners, a new organization founded in Minneapolis, Minnesota, is yet another organization that is radical about faith and work. Many of their members have

---

[6] *Leadership Network Explorer Lite #5,* February 28, 2000.

been instrumental in being involved in projects that feed the poor. Not long ago their members took containers of food and supplies to Indonesia and other countries. The co-founder of the organization, Dennis Doyle, owns one of the largest real estate companies in America. Nonetheless, his real passion is seeing lives changed through the power of Christ. He shares his personal testimony throughout the country with other business people.

There is now even an organization called the Avodah Institute that is expressly founded to address faith and work issues (avodahinstitute.com). Avodah Institute is a type of think-tank that encourages dialogue and education on the subject of work and faith integration. Still, another website entitled scruples.org was founded by Youth With A Mission missionary, Mike McLoughlin. His website was created to provide information to men and women in business about this movement taking place. News, articles, and information on micro-business and mission enterprises is a main focus of his website.

This movement is not just in America. In early 2000, the International Christian Chamber of Commerce (iccc.net) based in Sweden with more than 80 international chapters, launched a seven-week video series in China called, "You Can Start Your Own Business". Amazingly, this communist country asked this Christian marketplace organization to develop the course to be aired over their public broadcasting television system that has a potential audience of over 250,000 million viewers. Other international organizations such as Full Gospel Businessmen's Fellowship International and CBMC International have members throughout the world and are committed to reaching men and women for Christ in the workplace. This is truly a worldwide movement.

In the Fall of 1997, God led me to begin writing a daily meditation for fellow associates in the workplace via email. Each day I wrote a daily meditation and sent it off to those on my list. Soon others asked to be added. When the subscriber list got to 200, a friend and subscriber who owned a website called Goshen.net, nowcrosswalk.com, asked to help me by managing the subscription program and promoting it on his website. It began growing at 500 new subscribers a month. Soon it got to more than 27,000 subscribers worldwide and resulted in a book entitled *TGIF Today God Is First* which includes 365 individual meditations for those wanting to integrate their faith with their work (marketplaceleaders.org). Today the devotional is growing at more than 1000 new subscribers each month. At the same time, I began teaching a comprehensive workshop for men and women on understanding one's calling to the workplace, entitled *Called to the Workplace - From Esau to Joseph*.

All of this was yet another example of God's moving in the workplace. The response from men and women in the workplace throughout the world was another indication the movement was not just a U.S. movement, but a global movement.

Is there a move of God in the workplace today? The evidence reveals an overwhelming YES. However, I believe we are still in the early stages of this movement. (See complete listing of other work and faith resources in the back of this book).

Reflection

1.   The information in this chapter reveals the birth of many new ministries to the workplace. What do you think God wants to do through this?

2.   How do you think God might want these various ministries to work together and for what reason?

3.   God seems to be starting a worldwide movement. What might this mean for you in your own work situation?

CHAPTER

4

Where's The Impact on the Culture?

Therefore, go and make disciples of all nations, baptizing them in the name of the Father and of the Son and of the Holy Spirit, and teaching them to obey everything I have commanded you. And surely I am with you always, to the very end of the age" (Matt. 28:19-20).

Why is God calling forth his remnant in the church at this time in history? How effective has Jesus' church been in preaching and discipling the nations? If we answer this question based on the facts and the impact on the culture, we are left with some disappointing results. Since we are a global church, we must evaluate on a global basis. Obviously, our success is going to be different in different areas of the world. But the overall snapshot of where we are is not very positive. However, God is greater than statistics and He can change the picture in a blink of an eye. The problem is He is committed to using His people to impact the world. It is a partnership. Let's take a look at where we are in the world as far as penetrating the world with the gospel. Then, let's look at the United States and see the American church's impact on its culture.

Christianity in the World - "A Snapshot"

Of the global population of 6.091 billion, it is estimated that:

- 2.016 billion believe in Christianity in some form;

- 1.898 billion are members of Christian churches;

- 1.3 billion attend Christian services;

- 482 million belong to Pentecostal or Charismatic movements;

- 680 million are 'Great Commission Christians';

- In the year 2000, 165,000 will probably be martyred for their faith;

- There are 24,000 missions organizations which collect some US$120 billion per year;

- The total income of all church members is around US$12,700 billion, of which $220 billion are spent on Christian purposes;

- There are 5,104 million people in "full-time" ministry;

- The 4,000 Christian radio and TV stations are reaching a total of 2.15 billion people;

- 2 billion people live in poor urban areas, 1.3 billion of them in slums;

- There are 4,100 cities with over 100,000 inhabitants, 410 cities with over 1 million;

- Other religions and groups: 1.215 billion Muslims, 786 million Hindus, 774 billion non-religious, 362 million Buddhists, 225 million members of tribal religions, 152 million atheists, 102 million "new religious".[7]

Following is a summary of what these statistics mean in terms of our progress as cited by the International Bulletin of Missionary Research.

The twentieth-century expansion of the global Christian community is widely noted and celebrated - from half a billion people in the year 1900 to two billion in 2000. It is not as readily recognized that this remarkable expansion nonetheless has failed to translate into an increased percentage of the world's population. In his latest annual statistical table (see the January 2000 INTERNATIONAL BULLETIN) contributing editor David B. Barrett gives the Christian community as 33 percent of world population, little changed from what it was a hundred years earlier (actually slightly less). More remarkable than numerical expansion is the demographic shift in the global Christian community. In 1900, Christians in

---

[7] *Source: International Bulletin of Missionary Research, January 2000. David B. Barrett & Todd M. Johnson.*

Europe and North America accounted for more than 70 percent of the world Christian community, but at the end of the century these Christian heartlands contributed fewer than 40 percent. Today it is the non-Western world that boasts the majority-more than 60 percent of the globe's Christian population. Professor Robert attends to a peculiarity of this otherwise welcome phenomenon: even as the Christian faith has surged around the world, establishing what one would like to think of as a truly universal religion, close observers detect more fragmentation than ever. If mission leaders once worried about the divisiveness that Western denominations brought to their ministries in non-Western lands, what are we to think today when distinctives between Christian communities are further multiplied as indigenization plays itself out around the globe? As Robert writes, "What at first glance appears to be the largest world religion is in fact the ultimate local religion." In terms of the statistics Barrett has compiled over the years, there were fewer than 2,000 Christian denominations in 1900, 20,000 in 1980, and nearly 34,000 today. It is only right and fitting that we should rejoice at the global extent of Christ's followers, but as Robert challenges us, it is going to take diligent study and analysis if we are to appreciate just how all the parts fit into the impressive whole. This is a task alike for historians, theologians, and the practitioners of the world Christian mission.[8]

We must conclude from these statistics that although the church is growing, we are not keeping pace with the growth of the population in the world and our penetration from a percentage basis to the population is decreasing.

If you would like to learn more about this we encourage you to visit their website at http://www2.gospelcom.net/omsc/ibcurrnt.htm.

The U.S. Church

The indicators in the U.S. church are disturbing. For a nation that promotes itself as a Christian nation the impact of Christianity on the culture leaves us questioning how sincere our faith is since it has such little impact on the culture. The nation has seen disturbing trends such as increased crime in schools, a nation that continues to kill unborn children and a continued increase in pluralism with little regard for absolutes.

---

[8] *International Bulletin of Missionary Research* April 2000, Vol. 24, No. 2
http://www2.gospelcom.net/omsc/ibcurrnt.htm.

Consider this report from George Barna, a leading researcher on the church in the United States and other statistics cited from different sources.

"Our annual evaluation of the state of spirituality is in! Looking at nine key measures that we track every year, the keyword is continuity - there has been little change in people's religious behavior and beliefs, in spite of the evangelistic fervor displayed by some groups. Among the highlights of the study are:

- Born again Christians are 41% of the adult population - a figure that hasn't changed since 1995, but several percentage points higher than what was measured in the early nineties.
- Bible reading is the only measure to have increased appreciably in the past five years - but is still well below levels prior to the mid-nineties.
- Although thousands of churches are moving toward small groups or cell groups, the proportion of adults involved has remained stable since 1993."[9]

More Money Has Been Spent on Christianity With Less Impact

"Although churches in the U.S. have spent more than $530 billion dollars on ministry activities since 1980, the proportion of adults who are born again has remained virtually the same during the last 15 years."[10]

Very Little Growth in Christianity

1999: 40%
1998: 39%
1997: 43%
1996: 39%
1995: 35%
1994: 36%
1993: 36%
1992: 40%
1991: 35%[11]

---

[9] *Source: George Barna, email bulletin, March, 2000*

[10] 1995 Barna Research Study

[11] Barna Research Study

"The numbers of Americans who say they believe in God (86%) or a universal spirit (8%) and those who say they attended church or a synagogue in the past week (45%), are essentially the same today as they have been for decades."[12]

"The Christian church has stagnated, largely due to its comfort with routines and rituals that are neither challenging nor relevant for millions of people."[13]

A 1999 *USA Today/CNN Gallup Poll* survey found 40% of people pay more attention to their own views or the views of others than to God or religious teachings in deciding how to conduct life. The same poll found 44% say that many religions, not only Christianity, offer a true path to God.[14]

More Christians Divorce Than Non-Christians

Using statistics drawn from nationwide survey interviews with nearly 4000 adults, the data shows that although just 11% of the adult population is currently divorced, 25% of all adults have experienced at least one divorce during their lifetime. Among born again Christians, 27% are currently or have previously been divorced, compared to 24% among adults who are not born again.[15]

My wife works with Georgia Family Council, a state-based organization that promotes family-friendly legislation. In one of their studies they found that over half of 18-24 year olds in Georgia come from a divorced home.[16]

America has the highest number of single parent households among major countries 22.9%.

United States:	22.9%		UK:	12.7%
West Germany:	17.5%		Japan:	5.9%[17]
Canada:	14.8%		France:	10.9%

[12]-USA Today/Gallup Poll, Dec. '99

[13]-George Barna, After 1998 Survey of Impact of Churches on America.

[14] 1999 USA Today/CNN Gallup Poll

[15]-Barna Research, 1999

[16] 1998 Georgia Marriage Report

[17] Bureau of the Census report, 1992

"Today we have more Christians today per capita with less impact on the culture than ever before. We have more Christians today, but we are big and we are weak."

> Landa Cope, Dean of University of Nations, Youth With A Mission, October 1999.

More Americans claim to tithe than actually do.

17% of adults claim to tithe while 3% actually do so.[18]

Christians give only 2.5% of their money away.[19]

One Nation Under God?

- Only 12% of US adults read the Bible everyday.

- Americans are less interested in absolutes, preferring those perspectives which allow for relative values to gain credence. Absolutes will become less and less (Pluralism). This was demonstrated in 1999 by America's response to President Clinton's conduct which broke moral and legal laws with no consequence.

- The same poll found 44% say that many religions, not only Christianity, offer a true path to God.

Today, those in leadership are driven more by public opinion polls than what is right. We have shifted from leadership to pandering to the approval of others.

Secular Studies of Religious Behavior on the Workplace

In December 1983, The Princeton Religion Research Center published a landmark survey conducted for *The Wall Street Journal* by the Gallup Organization. The researchers

---

[18] (1997 Barna study)

[19] (*Christianity Today, 1987*)

measured a wide range of moral and ethical behaviors, such as calling in sick when not sick, cheating on income tax, and pilfering company supplies for personal use. The results were disappointing, to say the least.

But what the researchers found most startling was that there was no significant difference between the churched and the unchurched in their ethics and values on the job. In other words, despite the fact that more and more people attend churches, churches seem to be having less and less of an impact on the moral fiber of their people, at least in the workplace. To quote the researchers: "These findings...will come as a shock to the religious leaders and underscore the need for religious leaders to channel the new religious interest in America not simply into religious involvement but in deep spiritual commitment."[20]

Conclusions

"Either these are not the gospels, or we're not Christians," said Thomas Linacre, Henry VIII's doctor and Renaissance thinker, after given the four gospels in Greek. (Five years later Martin Luther hammered some church theses to a church door, and the Protestant Reformation began.) We could make this same statement today as we look at our own nation.

I believe Satan's number one strategy to defeat Christian business people is to make them ineffective in their business witness and to divide Christians by keeping them apart. His goal is to create disunity and division within the body of Christ. This is why many cite they would rather not work with a Christian businessperson. Satan is winning this battle. We need a paradigm shift within the body of Christ among business people. These findings reveal that our "church programs" are failing to impact the culture we live in. We all know that more data is not going to change the culture. Prayer, discipleship, unity, and a genuine move of God among God's people is the only catalyst to change a culture. It is not enough to know where we are in our impact; the real question is what are the reasons men and women are not impacting the culture because of their own relationship to God and what can be done to change this? We will look at this in the next chapter.

---

[20] Princeton Religion Research Center Study, 1983.

Reflection

1. What do the statistics reveal about the condition of the health of the church today?

2. How does this impact you personally?

3. What do you believe might be some reasons that contribute to us being in this condition?

5

Reasons For Our Lack of Impact

Earlier I described some of my own journey in coming to a greater awareness of God's move in the workplace. This has become a very personal journey for me and God has totally transformed my life because of this journey. By 1994, I had been a Christian for twenty years. I had been active as a Christian businessman for most of this time. But during the years following 1994, God began to show me why I had not been able to fully experience Christ in a powerful and intimate way that impacted others. I had believed myself to be very committed to Christ and had given ten percent of my income to the Lord's work. I had even personally led many people to Christ. However, there were some inconsistencies in my walk that I was not aware of until I experienced the crisis in 1994.

My discovery revealed that many Christian business people were ineffective in their Christian life for the same reasons that I had been ineffective. I realized that this was not due to an unwillingness to be used by God, rather, it was a result of other factors. In this chapter I want to review three primary causes why many Christians today fail to have an impact on their culture.

Reason #1: An Unbiblical View of Work and Ministry

Earlier we looked at the historical backdrop of why society and even the church have made a distinction between the secular and the sacred. We looked at the concept of "full time Christian work" versus those who worked in the secular arena. This is one of the major reasons why we have been ineffective. We have believed something about ourselves as men and women in the workplace that has not been Biblical. A dentist friend of mine once said that he was a disciple of Jesus Christ masquerading as a dentist. What a wonderful illustration of how I believe each of us should view our work lives. It does not mean we just place fish symbols on our letterhead or use other symbols to let others know we are Christians: rather, it is a way of life. Our work should have an overriding ministry objective to reflect Christ's love and power in our lives. More than 70% of our lives are spent working, whether that is in a formal marketplace position or serving as the vice president of internal affairs in a home full of children. We all work. However, many of us do not understand the holy calling that God associates with this work.

Fifty percent of Christians have never heard a sermon on work, and seventy percent have never been taught a theology of work. No wonder we have a difficult time reconciling the two concepts. We really have not been taught. What we have been taught has not been consistent with what God says about work, calling, and ministry. Our work is our ministry unto the Lord. *And whatever you do, whether in word or deed, do it all in the name of the Lord Jesus, giving thanks to God the Father through him* (Col 3:17). Later we will talk more specifically about work as a calling. For now, though, we need to begin to rid our vocabulary of terms that are so often misused and replace them with Biblical terminology. Here are just a few I would like to see removed from our vocabulary.

"Sacred and Secular" or "Religion Doesn't Belong in the Workplace."

God does not segment the sacred from the secular. God is involved in all areas of life.

Yours, O LORD, is the greatness and the power and the glory and the majesty and the splendor, for everything in heaven and earth is yours. Yours, O LORD, is the kingdom; you are exalted as head over all. Wealth and honor come from you; you are the ruler of all things (1 Chron 29:11).

"Only missionaries and preachers are in full time Christian Work."

We're all in full time Christian work, however, some are called to vocational ministry.

May the favor of the Lord our God rest upon us: establish the work of our hands for us—yes, establish the work of our hands (Ps 90:17).

"I'm Called to the Mission Field."

We're all called to the mission field. It is a matter of which mission field. There is no greater mission field than the marketplace. We must view this as a fertile field just as the overseas mission field is a fertile field. God wants to reach these people just as much as those who have not heard in foreign lands. Let's make sure we view life the way God views life. True, some are called to the "foreign mission field", but all are called to the mission field no matter what the landscape is like.

"I'm in the Ministry."

If you're not already in ministry, you won't be in it when you retire. Spirit-led ministry cannot be separated from a walk of faith.

We must not fall into this trap. Today, baby-boomers are focusing on the second half of life, but I have heard many men and women in business make statements like the one above. The problem is that if one is not already demonstrating fruit in their work life, they will not yield fruit after they have "retired" from their primary vocation. This too is a Greek philosophy of ministry that wants to segment the faith and work area of life.

A.W. Tozer, in his classic, *The Pursuit of God* says,

The 'layman' need never think of his humbler task as being inferior to that of his minister. Let every man abide in the calling wherein he is called and his work will be as sacred as the work of the ministry. It is not what a man does that determines whether his work is sacred or secular, it is why he does it. The motive is everything. Let a man sanctify the Lord God in his heart and he can thereafter do no common act. All he does is good and acceptable to God through Jesus Christ. For such a man, living itself will be sacramental and the whole world a sanctuary. His entire life will be a priestly ministration.[21]

---

[21] A.W. Tozer, *The Pursuit of God*, Christian Publications, Inc., 1948, p. 127, Harrisburg, PA.

Reason #2: The Church

Each of us has a particular experience as it relates to how we became a Christian. Some of us have had little church background and recently learned about Christ without prior knowledge. Others of us have been raised in the church. Regardless of which group describes you, each of us has had a particular influence as we have grown in our faith. For the next few moments, I would like you to take a self-assessment test. Please select which church experience based on two distinct models below best describes your experience. Be honest in your assessments.

Two Types of Church Experiences
Self-Assessment

Model 1	Model 2

❏ **Active** — appeals to the heart   ❏ **Cognitive** — appeals to the intellect
Has your experience encouraged you to focus your attention on developing a heart toward God, or has it focused more on Bible knowledge?

❏ **Process Focus**   ❏ **Program Focus**
Has your experience encouraged you to be a part of various programs in your church, or is there a continued focus on helping you relate to God through your personal relationship with Him as a process of growing in your intimacy?

❏ **Obedience As A Priority**   ❏ **Information As A Priority**
Has your church experience focused on obedience or information about God as a priority? Is there a cost to your obedience, or a belief without cost? Is Bible knowledge simply something to be shared instead of applied?

❏ **Relationships**   ❏ **Controlled Groups**
Has your church encouraged intimate and accountable relationships to be formed or is there more of a focus of controlled groups? Are there lots of programs that seem to have more emphasis than informal gatherings of believers?

❏ **Transparency, love**   ❏ **Service, activity-based**
Has your church experience encouraged the people to be transparent and vulnerable in their relationships with one another, or is there more of a focus on service within the church? Is genuine love and acceptance encouraged, or is toleration of others the norm?

Fruit	Fruit

❏ **Mature Believers**   ❏ **Shallow Believers**

Is there active participation or do you find a lack of interest in the activities of God? Is each believer trained to serve or are they trained professionals doing the work of the ministry? Do you see many believers active, or are there more spectators in your church?

Please tally your answers.

Which model did you most identify with?

<u>Model 1</u>	<u>Model 2</u>

❏ **Hebraic**   ❏ **Greek**

What I have just described for you are two different types of church experiences that most of us have experienced at one level or another. The left side describes the early, Hebraic church model. The right side describes a Greek model of church experience. The Hebraic model produces mature believers, whereas the Greek model produces shallow believers who tend to be more activity-focused in their relationship toward God.

In the early church there was an emphasis on developing a heart toward God. The relationship with God was the focus. God related to his people on a personal level. Obedience was the key to a healthy relationship with God. Decisions were not made based on reason and analysis, but by obedience. *The fear of the LORD is the beginning of wisdom; all who follow his precepts have good understanding* (Ps. 111:10). This is why many of the miracles performed in the Bible went against natural reason, (i.e., feeding five thousand, crossing the Red Sea, retrieving a coin from a fish's mouth, walking around Jericho to win a battle, etc.) God constantly wanted to check the leader's obedience, not his knowledge. Knowledge and reason came into the early church with the Greek scholars in subsequent centuries. This is when the church began to have more oratory skills accepted and encouraged. Gradually, over many centuries the focus on knowledge and reason has become more accepted in the church. This is why intimacy with God has been the fallout in many people's church experience. Their primary source of teaching and discipleship has been focused on the local pastor, instead of their personal walk and relationship with God and others in the body. In the early church, the rabbi was there primarily for quality control, not as the primary teacher and speaker. He did not even address the people from an elevated platform, but the whole congregation was in a more circular format. The focus was on the power of God working through each individual.

My message and my preaching were not with wise and persuasive words, but with a demonstration of the Spirit's power, so that your faith might not rest on men's wisdom, but on God's power (1 Cor. 2:4-5).

Block Logic

Marvin Wilson, author of *Our Father Abraham* has written extensively about the difference between the Hebrew view of faith compared to the more Greek view.

The use of what may be termed block logic is another important contour of Hebrew thought. Greek logic, which has to a large extent influenced the Western world, was different. The Greeks often used a tightly contained step logic whereby one would argue from premises to a conclusion, each step linked tightly to the next in coherent, rational, logical fashion. The conclusion, however, was usually limited to one point of view—the human being's perception of reality. By contrast, the Hebrews often made use of block logic. That is, concepts were expressed in self-contained units or blocks or thought. These blocks did not necessarily fit together in any obviously rational or harmonious pattern, particularly when one block represented the human thinking created a propensity of paradox, antinomy, or apparent contradiction, as one block stood in tension—and often illogical relation—to the other. Hence, polarity of thought or dialectic often characterized block logic.

It is particularly difficult for Westerners—those whose thought-patterns have been influenced more by the Greeks and Romans; than by the Hebrews—to piece together the block logic of Scripture. When we open the Bible, therefore, since we are not Orientals, we are invited, as Robert Martin-Achard states, to "undergo a kind of intellectual conversion" to the Hebraic world of the East." Let us turn, then, to some of the many examples of block logic found throughout scripture. The book of Exodus says that Pharaoh hardened his heart, but it also says that God hardened it (Ex. 8:15cf. 7:3). The prophets teach that God is both wrathful and merciful (Isa. 45:7; Hab. 3:2). The New Testament refers to Jesus as the "Lamb of God" and the "Lion of the tribe of Judah" (John 1:29, 36; Rev. 5:5). Hell is described as both "blackest darkness" and the "fiery lake" (Jude 13; Rev. 19:20):[22]

---

[22] Marvin Wilson, *Our Father Abraham*, P. 150, Eerdmans Publishing, Grand Rapids, MI 1989.

Jeremiah's Land Purchase

For this is what the LORD Almighty, the God of Israel, says: Houses, fields and vineyards will again be bought in this land (Jer. 32:15).

Jeremiah's land purchase is yet another example of this block logic. If I asked you to purchase some land when you knew that the country you were living in was about to be invaded and you were sure to be placed under arrest, how wise do you believe such an investment would be? Do you believe God would lead you to make such an investment? That is exactly what God told Jeremiah to do. However, God had a good reason for having Jeremiah make such a purchase. It was to be a testimony and a promise that God was going to restore the Jews to their land. It was a prophetic act on the part of Jeremiah. Friend, sometimes God may not allow us to use human logic in our decisions. Sometimes he leads us to make decisions that may not make sense to the world, or even those close to us. The key is knowing that God is leading us to make such decisions.

There are many more examples of this we could discuss. The important point here is to help you see that we as Westerners have looked through Greek glasses for most of our Christian experience and must make a paradigm shift in order to fully experience God in the way the early Hebraic church did. We cannot fully understand why God may lead us to make certain decisions. Our responsibility is simply to obey.

In the early church the emphasis was placed on relationships - with God and each other. If you recall Paul's admonition in 1 Corinthians 14 he said, *"What then shall we say, brothers? When you come together, everyone has a hymn, or a word of instruction, a revelation, a tongue or an interpretation. All of these must be done for the strengthening of the church"* (1 Cor. 14:26-27). The focus was on body ministry from and to one another. Each person was responsible for ministering to others within the body. The early church understood that knowledge was not what changed the word; it was the power of God working through people.

"For the kingdom of God is not a matter of talk but of power" (1 Corinthians 4:20).

"For we cannot help speaking about what we have seen and heard" (Acts 4:20).

If the early church made decisions based on the pro and con method of decision-making, there would be no miracles in the Bible. (i.e., such as getting the coin from the fish's mouth, walking around the walls of Jericho to take the city, Peter walking on water, etc).

I realized during my early spiritual journey that I had been a product of a Greek church experience. I experienced more emphasis on programs in my church experience instead of caring relationships and personal intimacy with God. This was only one of three important contributions to a lack of personal intimacy with God that resulted in a works-based relationship with God.

Reason #3: Subconscious Motivations

Jerry had grown up with a father who was a successful workaholic. Although Jerry lacked nothing materially, he felt a lack of closeness to his parents and had difficulty sharing his feelings with others as an adult. Then when Jerry was still in his early teens, his father died very suddenly. His large family was left with little support, and insecurity and fear became the dominating factors in the young man's life. Vowing to himself that he would never suffer financial need again, Jerry worked hard at his business in his adult life, putting stress on many personal and business relationships. He became very successful, however, a pattern began to emerge that motivated Jerry to place more restrictions on those around him when they failed in the financial area. His relationship with God was seen as a model among his peers, but when examined closer, there was something that just wasn't right. He often displayed times of anger in stressful situations and shamed his employees into the "correct" behavior. Jerry had little accountability beyond his clients. Finally, Jerry's marriage disintegrated and some major crises in his business led to financial difficulties. Through the counsel of some trusted friends and mentors who had a deeper understanding of spiritual strongholds, Jerry came to understand that underneath some of these symptoms was a spiritual stronghold that had been built in his life going back two generations. It was a stronghold of insecurity and fear that was manifested as control; control over people and circumstances. His need to protect became stronger than his desire to obey the voice of God in his life. When decisions had to be made that impacted him financially, he was often tempted to make an outcome-based decision instead of a purely obedience-based decision. As the Holy Spirit brought conviction of the sins he had committed against people in his life, Jerry purposed to seek forgiveness and make restitution. His priorities shifted to God and family, then close friends and business. God began to show Jerry that he could have true intimacy with God and others when these underlying strongholds were removed. Jerry became a new person who experienced, for the first time, a level of intimacy and freedom in his walk with God. Gradually, God began to lead him into a ministry that impacted the lives of others in the marketplace. Today,

Jerry sees the hand of God restoring all aspects of his life and can testify of God's miraculous hand in many of his everyday experiences in life and work.

The weapons we fight with are not the weapons of the world. On the contrary, they have divine power to demolish strongholds. We demolish arguments and every pretension that sets itself up against the knowledge of God, and we take captive every thought to make it obedient to Christ (2 Corinthians 10:4,5).

I am pleased to tell you that I am Jerry. This leads us to discuss the third reason I believe there are many people today who are not experiencing the intimacy and fruit of a healthy and powerful relationship with God. This one area, above all else, is the reason I believe there are many men and women today who really desire to impact their culture for Jesus Christ, but are hindered due to generational issues that have plagued their lives. However, the difficulty is that a stronghold works at the subconscious level, and is not easily recognized until a major crisis forces one to look deeper at the root causes of such problems.

Most Christian business people have a desire to follow and obey God, but there is something that prevents us from experiencing the full measure of God's love in our life. Paul prayed that we would experience this fullness.

I pray that out of his glorious riches he may strengthen you with power through his Spirit in your inner being, so that Christ may dwell in your hearts through faith. And I pray that you, being rooted and established in love, may have power, together with all the saints, to grasp how wide and long and high and deep is the love of Christ, and to know this love that surpasses knowledge—that you may be filled to the measure of all the fullness of God (Eph 3:16-18).

In Genesis 1 and 2 we find that God created us with the following six needs:

- Dignity
- Authority
- Security
- Purpose & Meaning
- Freedom & Boundary
- Intimate Love & Companionship

Whenever we seek to meet one or more of these basic needs outside God's design we have set the stage for the development of a generational stronghold.

You shall not bow down to them or worship them; for I, the LORD your God, am a jealous God, punishing the children for the sin of the fathers to the third and fourth generation of those who hate me, but showing love to a thousand [generations] of those who love me and keep my commandments (Exod. 20:5).

When I came into a greater understanding of the operation of spiritual strongholds, I did a thorough study of my family history. I interviewed family members to see what I could learn about the way my father and grandfather related to God and their families. I studied their work habits. I found that each of us had the same following symptoms.

- Need for recognition for performance. (i.e., Civic projects, sports, business success.)

- Emphasis on building financial security - workaholic.

- Lack of emotional intimacy.

- Activity-based relationship towards God - works.

- Over-control of people and circumstances.

This was an amazing discovery for me. For the first time, I realized this stronghold had impacted three generations of my family, and I was being given the opportunity to break this generational stronghold through the power of Christ, so that it would not get passed down any further.

Stronghold Development Process

Here is the way a stronghold develops in an individual. It usually follows this sequence.

1) Satanic-inspired THOUGHTS are introduced into one's mind.
2) Entertaining these thoughts brings on EMOTIONS.
3) Giving in to emotions eventually leads to taking some sort of ACTION.
4) Continual participation in this behavior causes one to develop a HABIT.
5) Once a habit is developed, a STRONGHOLD is built by that spirit.

It should be noted that strongholds *oppress* versus *possess*. They:

(1) Control, dictate, and influence our attitudes and behavior;
(2) Oppress and discourage us;
(3) Affect how we view or react to situations, circumstances, or people.

We overcome the influence of strongholds by renouncing and repenting of their influence through the prayer of faith in Jesus' blood to cleanse us from these influences. Francis Frangipane in his book, *The Three Battlegrounds*, describes what a stronghold is and how it works:

> ...the Apostle Paul enlists the word "stronghold" to define the spiritual fortresses wherein Satan and his legions hide and are protected. These fortresses exist in the thought-patterns and ideas that govern individuals and churches, as well as communities and nations. Before victory can be claimed, these strongholds must be pulled down and Satan's armor removed. Then the mighty weapons of the Word and the Spirit can effectively plunder Satan's house.

The Apostle Paul defines a stronghold as "speculation, a lofty thing raised up against the knowledge of God" (2 Corinthians 3:5). A demonic stronghold is any type of thinking that exalts itself above the knowledge of God, thereby giving the devil a secure place of influence in an individual's thought-life.

In most cases, we are not talking about a "spirit-possession." This author does not believe that a Christian can be possessed, for when a person is "possessed" by a demon, that demon fills their spirit the way the Holy Spirit fills the spirit of a Christian.

However, Christians can be oppressed by demons, which can occupy unregenerated thought-systems, especially if those thoughts are defended by self-deception or false doctrines! The thought, "I cannot have a demon because I am a Christian," is simply untrue. A demon cannot have you in an eternal possessive sense, but you can have a demon if you refuse to repent of your sympathetic thoughts toward evil. Your rebellion toward God provides a place for the devil in your life. Many believers have been taught that, because they have the Holy Spirit, they cannot be deceived. This also is untrue. One reason the Spirit of Truth was sent was because we so easily fall into self-deception. In fact, the very thought that a Christian cannot be deceived is itself a deception! Once that particular lie permeates a believer's mind, his ideas and opinions crystallize and remain in whatever state of spiritual immaturity he happens to be. All manner of spirits will attack the soul knowing they are protected by the armor of that person's own thoughts and doctrines![23]

I was recently having lunch with a staff member of Freedom in Christ Ministries founded by Neil Anderson. Neil has written extensively on the subject of spiritual strongholds and has helped hundreds of thousands of people gain freedom through the power of Christ. We were sharing our experiences about the influence of strongholds. Then, he made the following statement which I had been teaching in my seminars. "We have found that many churches attract similar strongholds in their congregations. We don't totally understand why this is, we just know it is true." I have had this same experience. I have noticed that the same stronghold can be found in a company. Likeminded strongholds attract one another. The primary stronghold of the marketplace is mammon (greed) and pride. A further study of this has revealed that even cities and nations have spiritual strongholds over them. Those who do spiritual warfare over cities find that they must understand the historical spiritual forces that have operated in that city before they can bring down such a stronghold and impact the city spiritually.

A Stronghold of Rebellion

James was a businessman who came into this discovery about generational strongholds after he had gone through a divorce. When working with James we discovered that he had a stronghold of rebellion in his life. We suggested James contact his mother and ask her what symptoms she saw in him without prompting her about the stronghold of rebellion. James pondered the idea, then phoned his mother, who lived out of state. Although he had maintained regular phone contact with her, he had always felt uneasy in her presence. She was sent a complete list of possible strongholds to review and was asked what she thought. "Our whole family has the stronghold of rebellion," she replied. As she scored James from 1 to 10 in intensity of symptoms, a picture emerged: strong will, stubbornness, independent spirit. James scored fairly low on strife and divisions and unteachableness. He called his brother and received scores almost identical to his mother's. Next came the real challenge: his ex-wife. She and James had maintained a friendly relationship during their years apart, and he knew he could trust her to be candid. Boy, was she candid! Her first scores were similar to his family's evaluations, but then she surprised him with high scores on strife and anger that leads to arguments. "Why?" he asked. "My family gave me low scores on those."

---

[23] Frances Frangipane, *The Three Battlegrounds,* Arrow Publications, 1989, p. 24,25 Cedar Rapids, IA.

She chuckled and said, "They weren't married to you." Then she asked if there was a category for pouting. During their marriage he had reacted to disagreements with silent frowns and distancing—behaviors that had carried into other relationships as well. James set the phone down and prayed, renouncing the stronghold of rebellion that had plagued him since childhood. A new desire to fully yield to God and to serve others flooded over him.

Following are just a few typical strongholds that can take root in our lives. This is an incomplete list. Prayerfully look over these key strongholds and see if you believe one or more of these may impact you. Freedom in Christ Ministries provides a helpful inventory booklet entitled *Steps to Freedom* by Neil Anderson that will allow you to identify and renounce specific strongholds.

Partial Listing of Strongholds

❑ Rebellion   ❑ Fear

❑ Pride   ❑ Heaviness/Depression

❑ Insecurity   ❑ Jealousy

❑ Sexual Impurity   ❑ Religiosity

❑ Control   ❑ Rejection

❑ Independence   ❑ Deceit

❑ Doubt   ❑ Doubt & Unbelief

❑ Anger

Note: See Steps to Freedom *booklet, Freedom in Christ Ministries for complete listing.*

The Angry Businessman

Imagine if you were born with a pair of sunglasses on and grew up looking at the world through those sunglasses. You would never know that you could see better without the sunglasses unless someone revealed this to you. Now imagine taking those glasses off for the first time and seeing the inside of a room much brighter and clearer. Strongholds operate this way. They masquerade as if they are our personality that we have accepted our whole life. However, the truth is when we come to Christ He wants to totally renew our mind and heart. The problem is getting restored to Christ's true nature in our lives.

A few years ago I was in the midst of a business deal with an associate named John. John was a good friend. We had to have a lawyer draw us a contract on a project we were involved with together. One day the lawyer called and said he was having problems working through the contract with John. It seems every time they would begin the process, John would react to the way the lawyer spoke to him. I recognized what was taking place and called John and told him I was going to drive an hour and a half away the next day to meet with him. When I arrived, I reviewed the project with John. "We have agreed on this, this and this. Right?" I said. "Yes, that is correct," said John. Then John began to complain about the lawyer and why he was having a problem. Then he got more upset the more he spoke about the situation. Finally, I interrupted and said, "In the name of Jesus I rebuke that spirit of insecurity and fear that is ruling over you right now. If you don't stop what you are doing right now I am leaving!" My friend was shocked. Frankly, I was shocked at my boldness. This is not my personality, but the situation was obvious to me. John was reliving the past hurts he had experienced at the hands of lawyers. He believed a lie about the situation and was being totally manipulated by old feelings. I explained further to him what was going on. He looked at me and said, "You are exactly right." We resolved the issue, signed the agreement and went on.

Understanding that a person may be operating through a stronghold is a helpful tool in relating to an individual. In the past I would have called John on the phone, shamed him into straightening up, and probably gotten angry to boot. The contract probably would have not been signed. But that is not what happened. God broke through in the Spirit and we were able to move forward.

There are literally millions of men and women in the workplace that are driven by subconscious motivations, or spiritual strongholds. God wants each and every one of them to walk free so that they might experience the full love and power of Jesus Christ in their lives. One of the major overriding strongholds is fear. Fear shows itself in so many ways. Fear of failure. Fear of loss of control. Fear of reputation. Fear of not having enough money. Fear of losing a job. Just about anything we do on a daily basis can have an element of fear. This is why it is important for each of us to connect with this side of our life.

Strongholds keep us from living for a cause greater than ourselves and become the primary motivation behind our actions. We become in bondage to them on a subconscious level. Space does not allow for an extensive study on the influence of spiritual strongholds. The stronghold listing is only a partial list of possible strongholds. I encourage you to give further study to this area if you feel that it may be impacting you or someone close to you. The steps to freedom from strongholds are as follows.

Steps to Freedom

1. Identify strongholds and their symptoms. Rank them from 1-10 by the level of influence they have. Work with someone close to you to confirm the strongholds. (i.e., spouse, close friend.)

2. Confess and renounce the influence of strongholds in Jesus' name. Each believer has the power of the Holy Spirit to renounce the influence of strongholds over their life. We "have divine power to demolish strongholds" (2 Corinthians 10:4).

Suggested Prayer

In the name and authority of the Lord Jesus Christ, we command Satan and all evil spirits to release me from the influence of

_____,_____,_____

so that I can be free to know and choose to do the will of God. As children of God seated with Christ in the heavenlies, we agree that every enemy of the Lord Jesus Christ be bound to silence. We say to Satan and all your evil workers that you cannot inflict any pain or in any way prevent God's will from being accomplished in my life. In Jesus' name. Amen

Suggested further study: *Steps to Freedom*, Neil Anderson; *Bondage Breaker*, Neil Anderson; *Living Free In Christ*, Neil Anderson, *Victory Over the Darkness,* Neil Anderson; *Freedom from Addictions*, Neil Anderson and Mike Quarles. *The Three Battlegrounds,* Frances Frangipane, Arrow Publications. Websites: www.ficm.org www.marketplaceleaders.org http://www.inchristsimage.org

Reflections:

1. Can you see why spiritual strongholds can prevent men and women from fully receiving all God has for them? Did you identify any strongholds for yourself in this chapter?

2. How might this information be used to allow more people to gain freedom in Christ?

3. God desires all people to be free in Christ. How do you see this information being used in your own life?

6

Called to the Workplace—Work as a Calling

"Then the LORD said to him, What is that in your hand?' 'A staff,' he replied" (Exodus 4:2). "But take this staff in your hand so you can perform miraculous signs with it" (Exodus 4:17).

The scriptures are full of symbols of work and God's activity in that work. In the above scripture, God took the symbol of Moses' work (shepherding) and said He was going to perform miracles with it. God wants to do the same in the lives of men and women throughout the world. The problem is we have been trained not to think that way. It is time for a paradigm shift in our thinking. We must understand that all of life is a partnership with God to reveal His love and power through every aspect of life—not just work, but all of life. When we make a decision to leave God out of certain aspects of life, God is grieved. He desires to reflect His glory in our lives—especially in our work life.

Gideon's Staff

With the tip of the staff that was in his hand, the angel of the LORD touched the meat and the unleavened bread. Fire flared from the rock, consuming the meat and the bread. And the angel of the LORD disappeared. When Gideon realized that it was the angel of the LORD, he exclaimed, "Ah, Sovereign LORD! I have seen the angel of the LORD face to face!" (Judges 6:21-22).

Gideon was a farmer who threshed wheat for a living using a staff or rod. This was commonly used in his day to beat out fitches and cummin (Isa. 28:27), but now it was being used for wheat. He was busy about his work when an angel of God appeared to him. The angel told him that he was going to be used to deliver the people of Israel from the Midianites who had been ravaging their land and crops for seven years because of Israel's disobedience. God was calling Gideon to do a new type of threshing. Instead of threshing wheat, he was being called to thresh the Midianites. God often calls men and women when they are in the middle of their marketplace activities performing honest work. Like Moses, Gideon received this word from God with reluctance and feelings of insecurity, citing that his family was of no stature to accomplish such a task. Regardless, God addressed Gideon as a "mighty warrior" (Judges 6:12). God often sees us for what we will become, not what we think we are. Once Gideon determines through a series of fleeces that it truly is God who is speaking to him, he does an interesting thing. He prepares an offering to the Lord of meat and bread. Once this offering is prepared, the angel uses the *tip of the staff* to consume the offering. Here God uses another symbol of his work to consummate a partnership to accomplish one of God's purposes in the nation of Israel. This time the staff is used to receive the offering presented to the Lord by touching the offering with the tip of the staff to consume it. God used the symbol of his work to ignite the fire that consumed the offering.

Gideon's Army

> The LORD said to Gideon, "You have too many men for me to deliver Midian into their hands. In order that Israel may not boast against me that her own strength has saved her...(Judges 7:2-3).

God has now placed a new calling on Gideon's life. He used his work as years of preparation for what he is now called by God to do. He is called to be a deliverer through the hands of God. Many in the marketplace who are called to deliver the oppressed and lost seek fulfillment through their careers and money. However, it is interesting the requirements God makes of Gideon. He must fight against an army of 135,000 (see Judges 8:8) and he wants to use 32,000 fighting men. Even this would be considered a seriously one-sided affair, but God tells him he has too many men and must pare them back to 300! Man, how do you like those odds? God tells him to use 300 to fight 135,000!

God gave Gideon a peculiar selection method for the 300 as he took the men down to the water. There the Lord told him, "Separate those who lap the water with their tongues like a dog from those who kneel down to drink" (Judg. 7:5b). What was the significance of this? Those soldiers who lapped water like dogs were soldiers who were more aware of the enemy around them compared to those who kneeled to drink. The lappers were men who were on constant guard to the danger around them, keeping their eyes up and looking about them. The others could be easily picked off.

If you and I are going to be one of God's elite, we must be ready for battle and sensitive to the spiritual dangers around us. We must be trained to go about our business while, at the same time, discern when the enemy of our souls is prowling about seeking to destroy us. "Be self-controlled and alert. Your enemy the devil prowls around like a roaring lion looking for someone to devour" (1 Pet. 5:8). Beware of the spiritual dangers around you. Ask God to make you one of Gideon's elite who is skilled and led by the Spirit to accomplish His purposes in this day.

Jesus Has Need of Your "Donkey"

As they approached Jerusalem and came to Bethphage on the Mount of Olives, Jesus sent two disciples, saying to them, "Go to the village ahead of you, and at once you will find a donkey tied there, with her colt by her. Untie them and bring them to me. If anyone says anything to you, tell him that the Lord needs them, and he will send them right away" (Matt. 21:1-3).

Donkeys represented commerce in the scriptures. It is interesting that Jesus chose to ride a donkey when He came into Jerusalem his final time. He had need of the donkey that day, and He still has need of your donkey. I was told recently that a donkey is the only animal that has a cross etched across its back that can be seen. Isn't that interesting? Centuries earlier there was another scripture that forecasted the relationship Jesus would have to a donkey. *He will tether his donkey to a vine, his colt to the choicest branch; he will wash his garments in wine, his robes in the blood of grapes* (Gen. 49:11).

Jesus is the choicest branch to tie our donkey to. The donkey is forever tied to the blood of the Lord Jesus. What keeps us from allowing our donkey to carry the love and power of Jesus throughout the marketplace? We're tied to the wrong tree. We must be willing to untie our donkey from the world's system and give the control of our "donkeys" to Christ.

Saul's Calling

God used a donkey to call the first king of Israel—King Saul. Saul was working for his father Kish. It seems that the family business used donkeys a great deal. On one occasion, several donkeys became lost. They were considered valuable enough to send Saul and a servant out to find them. This led Saul to eventually meet Samuel, the prophet, who told him his donkeys would be found, but he was there for a far more important reason. It is a fascinating story of a strategy God used to recruit Saul. (see 1 Samuel 9 & 10). Keep in mind that this is comparable to a modern-day business problem. Many times God uses a business problem to move us into a direction we never would have considered without such a problem. Let's face it, most business people are pretty hardheaded and need more serious prompting to move them into certain places with God.

Babylon: The Reason God is Calling Forth His Army

In Revelation chapter 17 and 18, we read of a future time in which Babylon will be judged. Babylon represents the world of commerce that is an anti-Christ system.

> When the kings of the earth who committed adultery with her and shared her luxury see the smoke of her burning, they will weep and mourn over her. Terrified at her torment, they will stand far off and cry "Woe! Woe, O great city, O Babylon, city of power! In one hour your doom has come!' "The merchants of the earth will weep and mourn over her because no one buys their cargoes any more-cargoes of gold, silver, precious stones and pearls; fine linen, purple, silk and scarlet cloth; every sort of citron wood, and articles of every kind made of ivory, costly wood, bronze, iron and marble; cargoes of cinnamon and spice, of incense, myrrh and frankincense, of wine and olive oil, of fine flour and wheat; cattle and sheep horses and carriages; and bodies and souls of men (Rev 18:9-13).

Notice that this scripture describes the fall of a system that will collapse in one hour. We live in a day when the world can easily change with the crash of any nation's stock market, and we have seen the effects of this upon the entire world.

My friend Peter Michell with the International Christian Chamber of Commerce in England provides further insight into Babylon and why God may be calling forth His men and women in the marketplace at this time.

We believe that the ruling power in the marketplace of this world is Babylon. This is shown in Revelation 17. A harlot rides a beast with numerous heads. We are told that the beast represents the kingdoms of the world, so there is a "harlot" system which rides on world governmental systems. Later, it becomes apparent that it is particularly the merchants—the businessmen and women who are affected by the downfall of Babylon.

In Ezekiel 28 Satan is described as the King of Tyre. Tyre is associated with trade (Ezekiel 28:5). Trade should be a great blessing to the world, but trade has been hijacked by the forces of evil. Money has become a God and a spiritual principality. All sorts of evil is practiced in the pursuit of money. Trade, which should be good and wholesome and a blessing to everyone, has been taken over in the pursuit of mammon and greed for one's own gain.

One man turns his eyes and his ambition away from the Lord and onto money, then, all sorts of evil practices flood in and the situation is ripe for demonic influence. The Lord is going to deal with this situation. In Revelation 17 and 18 we read of the downfall of Babylon—it seems that Babylon is described as both a harlot and a city! It's a bit confusing at first sight. It seems to me that the harlot, called "Mystery of Babylon," in Chapter 17, verse 5 is rather like a false bride for the antichrist. We know that Satan aspires to be in the position of God, and in his kingdom he will mimic the things of God. Therefore it should be no surprise to find the antichrist with a bride, and it should be no surprise that the bride is called both a woman and a city. For that is exactly what we find when we consider the bride of Christ. We, the church and the new Jerusalem are both called and described as the bride of Christ. This is because of the total association, one with the other, that is the church with the New Jerusalem, that they both carry the same title.

So it is with Babylon—the city (presently being reconstructed in Iraq by Saddam

Hussein) and the harlot are totally associated with each other in their opposition to God.[24]

As the time comes for Babylon to fall—and the process has already started—the marketplace will become more and more unstable, yet we are called to work and witness in the marketplace. This is not a time for getting out, rather it is a time for ensuring that we are hearing God on a personal basis. Now is the time when the Lord will work miracles among us. I believe there are two particular reasons for this. First, He wants us to demonstrate His power, and second, He is raising up Josephs among the children of God. In the time ahead there are going to be those used by God in the same way Joseph was used in Egypt—with wisdom and foresight in order to provide for the people. Joseph knew what was coming upon Egypt because he was given the ability by God to interpret dreams. He had wisdom because God gave him wisdom. The church needs people like this now and for the future - people who know the time and know what to do (Amos 3:7).

Calling Forth the Remnant

...men of Issachar, who understood the times and knew what Israel should do...
(1Chron 12:32).

In 1997, I was invited to South Africa for the Global conference on World Evangelism (GCOWE). More than 4,000 people from more than 130 nations were represented at this conference, which brought evangelical leaders and missionaries from around the world to determine how to reach the non-evangelized areas of the world. There was one major difference between this conference and all other such conferences - the marketplace was represented for the first time. There were several different "tracks" represented at this conference. It was the first time a business track was assembled. There were 550 men and women from approximately 50 nations around the world that came together to discover how God might want to use business to reach the unreached people groups of the world. It was an exciting time to see and hear God's remnant of the church that has largely been silent. For the most part, business people have been seen for the money they could give to missions, not what their hearts and minds could contribute.

It was the first time I had seen what I believe is a real live, modern-day "Joseph". I

---

[24] Peter Michell, *Anointing*, ICCC, p. 43, 44, London, England.

met some of the most incredible men who were humble, professional, and passionate about Jesus, who desired to see how God might use them to impact their world. I came away from that conference a changed man. I had to admit I had never met such men in my home country in the U.S. Not that they weren't there; I just hadn't met any of that caliber. Many things came from that conference that are still lasting fruit. The small nation of Benin, Africa, will never be the same as a result of Christian business people becoming involved in establishing the country as a Christian nation. God is calling out a remnant of His church which includes men and women who seek a greater use of their talent and resources to impact the Kingdom of God, and many of them are impacting the nations because they have the respect of those where paid clergy will never gain access.

Made to Fly

Gunnar Olson, the founder and president of the International Christian Chamber of Commerce, has had a profound impact on my life. I must credit Gunnar for being the catalyst God used to help me see there is a difference when God is released fully in a person's work life. I saw and experienced in Gunnar a man who expected to see signs and wonders accompany his walk with God in the marketplace. His life has been an affront to my spiritual paradigm. I have never been the same since!

Gunnar likes to tell the story about the egg. "An egg was made to fly," he often says. "But before it can fly there has to be a transformation. The egg must hatch, grow wings and then be tossed out of the nest to be forced to fly." Gunnar correlates the spiritual transformation in the businessperson to this type of transformation within the egg. We are all made to fly spiritually, but unless we become transformed in our minds and our nature, we will never achieve what we were designed for in God. The following process has become an important understanding of the spiritual pilgrimage many of us will have to go through. It was in my first meeting with Gunnar Olson in 1996 that he shared the core principles of these stages of the journey. After he shared the basic concept, God began to reveal many other aspects of this journey that I now share with men and women in the workplace.

The First Stage

Precious in the sight of the LORD is the death of his saints (Ps 116:15).

When a Christian in the workplace makes a decision to live for Christ he receives a new heart. Up to this point, he has been operating more in an Egyptian or Babylonian

Esau to Joseph Recruitment Process

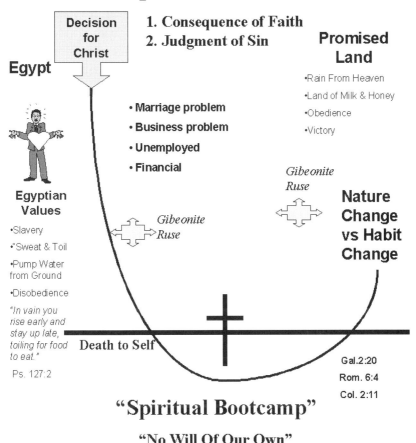

Decision for Christ

Egypt

1. **Consequence of Faith**
2. **Judgment of Sin**

Promised Land
- Rain From Heaven
- Land of Milk & Honey
- Obedience
- Victory

- **Marriage problem**
- **Business problem**
- **Unemployed**
- **Financial**

Gibeonite Ruse

Nature Change vs Habit Change

Egyptian Values
- Slavery
- "Sweat & Toil
- Pump Water from Ground
- Disobedience

"In vain you rise early and stay up late, toiling for food to eat."

Ps. 127:2

Gibeonite Ruse

Death to Self

Gal.2:20
Rom. 6:4
Col. 2:11

"Spiritual Bootcamp"

"No Will Of Our Own"

* Special thanks to ICCC for use of this diagram.

system of work. This system was best represented through sweat and toil to pump water from the earth. Most of us have sweated and toiled to build our businesses. In this case, we have been enslaved by a taskmaster --- our work.

Upon receiving Christ, we find God beginning a new process. For some this process is due to their own sin of adopting the Egyptian lifestyle of greed, idolatry, and independence. For others, it is merely a consequence of their faith. In either case, the process is similar. God begins to strip away all the things that do not contribute to their Christlikeness.

This painful, but necessary process often involves great adversity for a period of time. The greater the calling, often the greater the adversity. This is because of the message God desires to speak through this person. It is spoken of in Hosea 2:14-20 as a desert experience in which God sets us aside and speaks tenderly to us. It is interesting to note that the word "desert" actually comes from a Hebrew word that means, "to speak." The desert is a place of solitude, limited resources and time to think. It is also referenced in Isaiah 45:7. This process is designed to create a "no will of our own" attitude, much like boot camp is designed to do.

I tell you the truth, unless a kernel of wheat falls to the ground and dies, it remains only a single seed. But if it dies, it produces many seeds (John 13:24).

At some point, the individual becomes dead to his own interests, which really is the goal of the Christian life. God wants us "dead" so that His life can be fully lived through us. This death process is called "circumcision" for every believer in Jesus Christ. Circumcision is painful, bloody and very personal. It is in the successful passage through this process that the person becomes the most useful to God. The person begins to experience the fullness and the power of Jesus Christ once this process is complete. Paul describes the process in Romans 6:4, *...just as Christ was raised from the dead through the glory of the Father, we too may live a new life.* Often the person becomes more successful in their work life after this process, although this should not be construed as a formula for success. I remember having lunch with a mentor one time in the early stages of this process. He said, "If I could 'shoot' you, I would. You will be so much happier when you 'die'." This man knew what a life was like that was dead to the old life. He wanted me to experience it, but I was slow to die. The old, carnal nature still wanted to live on.

The Gibeonite Ruse

The heart is deceitful above all things and beyond cure. Who can understand it?
(Jer. 17:21).

During this process, the person is often presented with several Gibeonite Ruses that are designed by Satan to take him off this important path. This phrase refers to the time Joshua and the people were traveling through the Promised Land and came upon the Gibeonites. Because the Gibeonites were fearful of Joshua and his people, they tricked them into believing that they too were travelers in the land. The Bible tells us that Joshua did not inquire of the Lord about the Gibeonites. This led to Joshua and his people making a peace treaty with the Gibeonites. This was not pleasing to the Lord and resulted in the Gibeonites being enslaved by Israel. The result was Joshua and the people had to manage the Gibeonites and many intermarried with the clan. This was never supposed to have happened because God instructed Joshua and the people to wipe out their enemies completely.

The Gibeonite Ruse in business shows up in the form of a get rich quick scheme that claims to alleviate our problems, or some other meaningful opportunity. This distraction gets the person off track for what God is trying to accomplish through this process. However, if the person goes through this process and a change of nature is accomplished, they will never be the same. They will see much fruit in their lives. If they simply change some habits, they will go around the mountain again. All of us are susceptible to the Gibeonites Ruses in our lives the minute we begin to operate on our own reasoning. This example provides an encouragement to us to keep our vertical focus on walking with God on a daily and even moment-by-moment basis.

When a person begins a life of obedience they begin to understand the difference between living in Egypt as an Esau versus living in the Promised Land as a Joseph. They learn that their obedience is the key to provision, not sweat and toil. They learn that God blesses obedience, many times spiritually and physically more than before the crisis. A Joseph is one who is both a provider spiritually and materially.

Many in the Bible experienced this process. Those who had great anointing also experienced great adversity, i.e. Abraham, Moses, Elijah, Joseph, Paul, David, and Peter. Many business leaders such as R.G. LeTourneau and J.C. Penney went through the same type of experiences. Both R.G. LeTourneau and J.C. Penney experienced failed businesses before they became truly successful spiritually and professionally.

The Rebuilding Process

Unless the LORD builds the house, its builders labor in vain. Unless the LORD watches over the city, the watchmen stand guard in vain (Ps. 127:1).

The Foundation

Once the circumcision of the heart takes place, a rebuilding must take place. It helps to compare this process to the building of a house. Before the house can be built, we must go below the surface in order to find the bedrock on which to build. This bedrock for the Christian must be Jesus Christ and Him alone. Once the bedrock is established, next comes the porous rock that is poured on top of the foundation to allow water to be drained. This porous rock represents the deeper work of the Holy Spirit resulting in greater faith experiences.

Faith Experiences

> *"Whoever has my commands and obeys them, he is the one who loves me. He who loves me will be loved by my Father, and I too will love him and show myself to him"* (John 14:21).

These faith experiences are those times that we experience God at a deeper level than ever before. For example, when the people of Israel crossed the Jordan, this was a faith experience they will always remember as a day God revealed Himself personally to them through a miracle. They marked this day with 12 stones along the river. The width and depth of these faith experiences are directly proportional to the calling God has on our lives. The greater the calling, the greater the faith experiences.

One of my major faith experiences was when I discovered the meaning of my name had a direct relationship to Esau in the Bible. I had been studying the relationship of Esau to Christians in the workplace leading up to this discovery. This was a "burning bush" moment for me that helped confirm my call to help free men and women in the workplace from the "Esau life" and fulfill their calling in the workplace. God demonstrated His involvement in many other tangible ways that became faith experiences. These faith experiences encouraged my faith and the faith of others who heard my stories. God desires to build a testimony through every person's life.

The Building Process

1. Establish the foundation.

2. Faith Experiences (spiritual markers).

3. Motives of the heart.

4. Skill ability, and quality to perform the task.

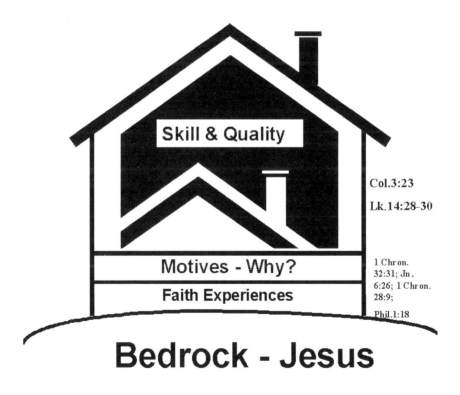

Motives

All a man's ways seem innocent to him, but motives are weighed by the LORD (Prov. 16:2).

Next, we must evaluate our motives. Why are we doing what we are doing? Is our motive pure? Are we responding out of obedience, or are other motives driving our decisions? Perhaps our motive is purely financial. Perhaps it is related to power or prestige. These motives will not stand. There is a motive behind everything we do. We must make sure the motive is the motive that God will bless.

The Promised Land is signified by a land that flowed with milk and honey because of the rain from heaven. There is no sweat and toil required, only obedience. Obedience insures provision. Sometimes it is more than we deserve; sometimes it is less than we want. This is the place God wants each of us. We need to understand what it means to walk in obedience and allow provision and success to be the fruit of our obedience, not a goal unto itself. When obedience becomes more important than outcome, it is a sign you are beginning to grasp the principle of entering the Promised Land in your work life. This is a motive God will always bless.

Therefore everyone who hears these words of mine and puts them into practice is like a wise man who built his house on the rock. The rain came down, the streams rose, and the winds blew and beat against that house; yet, it did not fall, because it had its foundation on the rock. But everyone who hears these words of mine and does not put them into practice is like a foolish man who built his house on sand. The rain came down, the streams rose, and the winds blew and beat against that house, and it fell with a great crash. By the grace God has given me, I laid a foundation as an expert builder, and someone else is building on it. But each one should be careful how he builds (Matt. 7:24-27).

Quality and Ability

Whatever you do, work at it with all your heart, as working for the Lord, not for men, since you know that you will receive an inheritance from the Lord as a reward. It is the Lord Christ you are serving (Col. 3:23,24)

Finally, we are ready to raise the building. In order to do this we must seek to be skilled in what we do. Do we have the skill, ability, and quality to perform the tasks? If not, the shingles will be crooked, the door jams will not match; the roof will leak. Many Christians have good motives and solid foundations but lack the experience to carry out the job. Conversely, many Christian business people have been skilled in their jobs, but lack the spiritual depth to avoid pitfalls due to wrong foundations and wrong motives of the heart.

Reflection

1. Where are you in the process described above? Do you believe you have fully given over your life to God's purposes?

2. Has God allowed a crisis in your life? If so, He may be taking you through the circumcision process. Ask God to show you.

3. What is necessary for you to experience God in a greater way in your life and work?

7

The Joseph Calling

When I met Gunnar Olson in 1996 and he explained the Joseph Calling to me, it was like a heavy weight was lifted from my shoulders. For the first time I saw my circumstances in a new light, and no longer saw them as something "I did" that was the reason for my problems. Sure, I had not been perfect in my life, but the kinds of problems I was experiencing were much larger than the mistakes I may have made in comparison. I know that some who will read this book have also gone through great adversity in their lives. Perhaps you have not been able to make sense of it all. Perhaps you are a modern-day Joseph. In this chapter, I want to briefly explain the Joseph Calling and why Joseph was required to go through the adversity he did.

Who Was Joseph and What Prepared Him For His Calling?

The meaning of the name Joseph is "God will increase," "May He Add" and "Increaser." When the Bible speaks of Joseph, it says that God was aware of his plight and that God was blessing Joseph. *The LORD was with Joseph and he prospered, and he lived in the house of his Egyptian Master* (Genesis 39:2). Even though he was a slave, God described him as being prospered by God.

> *He called down a famine on the land and destroyed all their supplies of food; and he sent a man before them—Joseph, sold as a slave. They bruised his feet with shackles, his neck was put in irons, till what he foretold came to pass, till the word of the Lord proved him true* (Psalms 105:16-19).

Joseph's "boot camp", which took 13 years, required separation from his former life, having his will and ability to control anything taken away, a breaking of his will, and a continued confrontation of his own crisis of belief that God was a loving God and that He was still in control of the events in his life. Here are a few facts about the life of Joseph.

He was

- sold into slavery by his own brothers.

- wrongfully accused and imprisoned for a crime he did not do.

- sexually pure.

- continually serving others who could have spoken up to get him out of prison, in spite of the fact he stayed two more years.

- not guilty of any sin and never cursed God for his circumstance.

- one who lived a righteous life amidst a heathen culture with continued pressure to conform to its lifestyle.

- reminded again and again that God was with him, meaning that God was the orchestrator of all this hardship. He had continued affirmations from God that God was PROSPERING JOSEPH.

- promoted by God supernaturally, but he never viewed himself as the owner of the resources of Egypt, only an administrator.

- able to understand authority and the importance of giving deference to those above him.

- blessed with an understanding of the omnipotence of God in his life.

- gifted to operate in the realm of the supernatural direction of the Spirit such as dreams, prophecy, words of wisdom and knowledge, administration and prayer.

- a provider both spiritually and materially.

- kept in "prison" as long as necessary to complete the work in Joseph - no more, no less than required.

Joseph was a type of Jesus. He suffered for those he would ultimately save. He was rejected by His own people. He provided spiritually for those he was called to serve. God invested a lot into Joseph for this special calling. That calling would save an entire nation and world from starvation. He would be one of the youngest rulers ever in history at age thirty. God could not afford to have a man in this position with any pride. His years of testing and toiling were designed to remove any vestiges of pride in his life. My friend Bob Mumford once said the following statement that I entirely agree with. "Beware of any Christian leader who does not walk with a limp."

Four Tests

God took Joseph through four unique tests. I personally believe that he was required to pass each test successfully before he qualified for the next. After each successful test he was given another. Finally, he passed the last one and was elevated for the call that God ultimately had on his life.

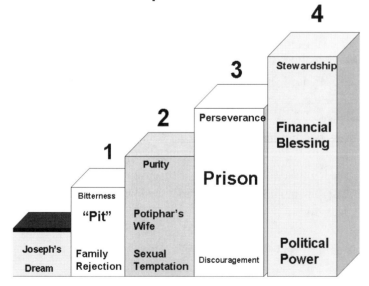

Each of Joseph's 4 Tests Moved Him Toward Fulfillment of God's Ultimate Purpose for His Life

"...til the Word of the Lord proved him true." (Ps.105:19)

Graduate Level Faith

See to it that no one misses the grace of God and that no bitter root grows up to cause trouble and defile many (Heb 12:15).

Joseph's first test was his family's rejection. He was sold as a slave to traders. What could be worse than to have your own family sell you into slavery? Betrayal is one of the most difficult tests in life. It would be very easy to fall into bitterness toward your family and God if something like this happened to you. Everyday you and I must work in a marketplace that does not treat its employees and vendors in an honorable manner. Sometimes, its downright cruel. Some of the most difficult hurts come from our own family members or those in the body of Christ. I believe some of these experiences are actually allowed in our path in order to find out how we are going to handle them. A.W. Tozer said, "It is doubtful whether God can bless a man greatly until he has hurt him deeply." Almost every leader I know who God has used has experienced a Judas type of betrayal at one time or another in their life. Whether God elevated them was dependent on how they handled the situation. I believe this is God's graduate level course in a walk with God.

I recall when a Christian client had fired us as their agency. They also left a balance owed to us of more than $140,000. They disputed the balance with us because of a problem that arose with a project we did. We did all we could to solve the problem and ate considerable costs, yet it was not satisfactory to the client. I sued the company, but a few months later the Lord showed me I was to drop my suit and even eat the outstanding balance. It was a painful but necessary obedience test. I dropped the suit and it took me about five years to pay off creditors related to the account. I forgave the man and even took him out to dinner shortly after I dropped the suit.

Bitterness and unforgiveness have disqualified many a person from moving on in God. God will not elevate you if there is any root of bitterness in your life. If you have something against a brother or sister, you must make it right if you expect God to bless your life.

The Place of Strength

So Abram moved his tents and went to live near the great trees of Mamre at Hebron, where he built an altar to the Lord (Genesis 13:18).

One day Abraham and his nephew Lot realized that the land they were living on could no longer support both families and all their flocks. It was decision time. They were going to have to split up. This meant someone had to go a different direction. But who should get first choice of the land? Obviously, Abraham was Lot's senior and by all rights should have that choice. Abraham could have pulled rank on Lot since he was the elder. This story is the model for splitting a business partnership. However, few businesspeople are willing to follow Abraham's example.

Abraham took a totally different approach to solving this problem. He told Lot to choose which land he wanted. Imagine, Abraham could have been dooming himself and his family if he was unable to find adequate land and water for them. He gave up his rights in the matter, and Lot took full advantage. "Lot looked up and saw that the whole plain of the Jordan was well watered, like the garden of the Lord, like the land of Egypt, toward Zoad (Gen. 13:10). So Lot left and took up residence in the valley later to be known as Sodom and Gomorrah. Sometimes what seems good on the front end turns out to be disastrous later. Such would be the case for Lot and his family.

As for Abraham, he made a choice. He decided to take life's high road choice that didn't necessarily mean it would benefit him. He was willing to leave that outcome to God. He made the decision based on an eternal measuring stick. Interestingly, the place where Abraham moved was called Mamre. In Hebrew, the name Mamre means "strength." How can choosing the weakest position become "strength"? Jesus must have asked the same question of His Father when faced with the proposition of going to the cross. How can the cross be a place of strength? The devil thought he had won, but the cross is what freed the captives for eternity. The Bible tells us that when we are weak, then we are really strong. To willingly choose the way of the cross becomes our strength.

I had a vice president who left my company during the greatest time of my trials. He decided to leave the company and take my second largest account. I had a non-compete agreement with him. After a great deal of prayer and counsel, I decided to release this man to pursue my client if he felt that was what he should do. I told him I did not agree with what he was doing, but I would not enforce the non-compete agreement. When Jesus said love your enemies, I believe He meant it. God took care of me, but I did lose the account and I know God wanted me to release this man and release the outcome into His hands.

A few years later I had a very close friend who had become a mentor to me. We were best of friends. However, an issue arose in our relationship that turned out to be very negative. It was so painful. I never imagined that a relationship could go from being so good one day, to being so bad in another. However, God used this situation to show me exactly how He must have felt when Judas betrayed him. It was one of his closest companions. Jesus wants to know whether we are willing to wash the feet of Judas.

Purity

Don't let anyone look down on you because you are young, but set an example for the believers in speech, in life, in love, in faith and in purity (1Tim 4:11-13).

The second test for Joseph was in the area of moral purity. Imagine being in the court of Pharaoh's house and being continually exposed to beautiful women walking around in the palace. Joseph had not been around women for a long time. To make matters worse, the most beautiful and powerful of them all begins to make passes at Joseph. This is a huge test for any man. However, Joseph was found faithful in this test. He did the only thing a man can do to withstand sexual temptation—he fled. You cannot overcome sexual temptation in any other way. The minute you start playing with it, it will eventually take you down. So men, heed this warning: stay away from compromising situations. You do not want to be disqualified because of failure in this area. If you are tempted through your computer, make sure you get it "sex-proofed" so that you are not faced with this temptation.

Perseverance

But when all goes well with you, remember me and show me kindness; mention me to Pharaoh and get me out of this prison (Gen 40:13-14). *The chief cupbearer, however, did not remember Joseph; he forgot him* (Gen 40:23).

The third test for Joseph was perseverance. Joseph had been in prison many years. He now had the opportunity to interpret a dream for some powerful folks--people who could deliver him from his pit. It is clear that Joseph had his hopes up, but he was not released. He remained in prison for another two years. It is at this point many would give up the fight. They would even consider taking their own lives. Scripture says that hope deferred makes the heart sick (Prov. 13:12). Joseph was probably sick, but there was something inside of him that kept him going. He persevered. Samuel Rutherfod once commented, "Praise God for the hammer, the file, and the furnace. The hammer molds us, the file shapes us, and the fire tempers us."

This is one of the most difficult aspects of the Joseph process. I was in that process for six years. At one time, I had a staff of seven. Then, when my world fell apart, I was by myself for five years. No secretary. No one in my office. I was alone and forced to do the best I could to satisfy creditors and make ends meet. At times, it seemed like a never ending treadmill, but God was doing a deeper work than I could see at the time. He was building character. He was removing pride. He was preparing me for something handtailored for me. This process is the one I find many business people cannot wait on. So often, they will move when God says stand still and wait. We decide that we have been in this place long enough, so we set out to deliver ourselves. That is a big mistake. Because if God has not completed the deeper work, He will take you around the mountain one more time --even more times if that is what is necessary to complete the inner work He wants in your life. Persevere my friend and see the deliverance in God's time, not your own. You will be blessed if you do.

Stewardship

So Pharaoh said to Joseph, "I hereby put you in charge of the whole land of Egypt" (Gen. 41:41-42).

Joseph is finally freed from prison when he is elevated to the second highest position in Egypt, but it is a funny thing. Once you have lived in a difficult state for a long time and you have become "satisfied" that you can live in that state, your elevation does not mean that much. I believe this was probably the case for Joseph. He had become dead to his circumstances.

R.T. Kendall describes where He believes Joseph was emotionally and spiritually at the time of his elevation.

When the time came for God to fulfill Joseph's dreams, Joseph himself had virtually no interest at all in it. Jesus said, "For whoever wants to save his life will lose it, but whoever loses his life for Me will save it" (Lk. 9:24). God wants to teach us a different set of values so that the kind of thing we start our wanting becomes secondary. God has something in mind for us that is far greater than the interest we began with.

Joseph's day of exaltation had arrived. Yet, through it all, a very real humiliation had to take place. We know about the humiliation Joseph had experienced for 13 years after being sold by his brothers into slavery, and then taken to Egypt. We know how he was falsely accused and cast into prison.

Then came a different situation. Joseph had had a triumph and was given exaltation, but the kind he never asked for. He did not appear to be all that interested in what was about to happen. He watched as the Pharaoh took his ring off his finger and put it on Joseph's finger. Joseph never asked for that. All he wanted was to go home. He longed to go back to Canaan, to see his father, and to have his dreams fulfilled.

Therefore, here we find an extraordinary incongruity: a humiliation in the heart of vindication. A triumph that was the opposite of everything he, himself, could have envisaged. Joseph wanted to go home, but a one-way ticket to Canaan wasn't available. Before he knew it, he had Egypt in his hip pocket. He had never prayed for that. But God wanted Egypt. What God wanted is what Joseph got. Joseph was given something that he could be trusted with because it didn't mean that much to him.[25]

Joseph performed well in his new role. He was a good steward. Oswald Chambers once said, "Not every man can carry a full cup. Sudden elevation frequently leads to pride and a fall. The most exacting test of all to survive is prosperity." In the case of Joseph, we know he passed the most exacting test of all.

---

[25] R.T.Kendall, *A Treasury of Wisdom Journal* (Uhrichsville, Ohio: Barbour and Companu, 1996), January 16 day reading.

Reflection

1. How has this chapter helped you to understand the role of adversity in the Joseph Calling?

2. If someone were going through a difficult time, how might you be able to help them based on what you read in this chapter?

3. God is calling forth many modern-day Josephs today. Do you believe you are one of them? Do you know of others who might be?

8

Called to Impact the Culture

Jesus replied: "Love the Lord your God with all your heart and with all your soul and with all your mind.' This is the first and greatest commandment. And the second is like it: 'Love your neighbor as yourself.' All the Law and the Prophets hang on these two commandments (Matt 22:37-40).

There are many men and women who have made spiritual discoveries that resulted in being used by God to impact their world. This is the ultimate fulfillment when a person understands they are actually called to the work they are doing and God uses them to impact their world. True success is fulfilling the purpose for which God made you. It has little to do with money, prestige or notoriety. God's measurement of success is very clear - doing the will of God. His greatest commandment is to love the Lord your God with all your heart, soul and mind. From this relationship with God everything else should flow. We cannot help but impact our culture if we love God and obey Him.

A New Kind of Business Person

They chose Stephen, a man full of faith and of the Holy Spirit: also Philip, Procorus, Nicanor, Timon, Parmenas, and Nicolas from Antioch, a convert to Judaism (Acts 5:6).

God is raising up a new remnant of men and women in the workplace that perform their work with an overriding ministry objective to it. Our first model of this kind of man was Stephen. In the book of Acts, we learn that the disciples needed to expand their leadership base and make more time for personal study of the scriptures. They decided to appoint others to handle a special food distribution program that was suffering because there were not enough people to service the need. The answer was to appoint more leaders to take this responsibility. Stephen was one of those appointed who was also a businessman. He also had some other characteristics spoken of in chapter 6: *Now Stephen, a man full of God's grace and power, did great wonders and miraculous signs among the people* (Acts 6:8). Not long after the disciple laid hands on these men revival began to spread beyond Jerusalem. As with most moves of God, opposition arose when the power of God began to be manifested through Stephen. Not so surprisingly, it came first through the religious community. Stephen preached to the people and became the first martyr as a result. In fact, it was Stephen and the other marketplace disciples who were the catalysts to take the message beyond the borders of Jerusalem while the disciples remained in the city.

Over the last few years God has allowed me to bump into more and more men and women who understand what it means to live for a cause greater than themselves. They see their "staffs" as something God wants to use to perform miracles. There have been many such men and women who have used their marketplace experience to impact their cultures. Here are just a few of them at different periods of history.

Brigid of Ireland

Brigid was born from a sexual encounter between an Irish king and one of his slaves in the fourth century. She was reared as a slave girl within the king's household and was required to perform hard work on the king's farm. From the beginning, Brigid took notice of the plight of the less fortunate. She would give the butter from the king's kitchen to working boys. She once gave the king's sword to a passing leper---an act about which the king was enraged. The king tried to marry her off, but to no avail. One day, Brigid fled the king's house and committed herself to belonging only to Christ.

Brigid sought other women who also wanted to belong only to Christ. Seven of them organized a community of nuns that became known as the settlement of Kildare, a place where many thatch-roofed dwellings were built, and where artist studios, workshops, guest chambers, a library, and a church evolved. These and other settlements became little industries all to themselves, producing some of the greatest craftmanship in all of Europe. Many of the poor had their lives bettered because of Brigid's ministry to them. Brigid became a traveling evangelist, helping the poor and preaching the gospel. When she died in 453, it is estimated 13,000 people had escaped from slavery and poverty due to her Christian service and industry. Her name became synonymous with the plight of the poor. She was a woman who turned a life of slavery and defeat into a life lived for a cause greater than herself. She became a nationally known figure among her people, and the Irish people still recognize her each February 1.

William Wilberforce

In 1787, William Wilberforce was known as "the greatest moral achiever of the British people," as stated by biographer John Pollack. Wilberforce was attributed with demolishing the slave trade in England and sixty-nine different initiatives that had worldshaping significance. Wilberforce came to faith in 1785 at the age of twenty-five. As a result, he began to think that spiritual matters were much more important than secular matters. However, a converted slave trader named John Newton, who also authored the famous hymn, *Amazing Grace,* convinced Wilberforce that he could have greater impact as a politician than as a minister. After much consideration and prayer, he agreed. He wrote these words in his journal in 1788: "My walk is a public one, my business is in the world; and I must mix in the assemblies of men, or quit the post which Providence seems to have assigned me." Wilberforce impacted his culture more than any man of his time.

Jeremiah Lanphier

Jeremiah Lanphier was a businessman in New York City who asked God to do something significant in his life in 1857. In a small darkened room, in the back of one of New York City's lesser churches, a man prayed alone. His request of God was simple, but earthshattering: "Lord, what wilt Thou have me to do?"[26]

He was a man approaching midlife without a wife or family, but he had financial means. He made a decision to reject the "success syndrome" that drove the city's businessmen and bankers. God used this businessman to turn New York City's commercial empire on its head. He began a businessmen's prayer meeting on September 23, 1857. The meetings began slowly, but within a few months, 20 noonday meetings were convening daily throughout the city.

---

[26] John Woodbridge, ed., *More Than Conquerors* (Chicago, Illinois: Moody Press, 1992), 337.

The New York Tribune and the *New York Herald* issued articles of revival. It had become the city's biggest news. Now a full-fledged revival, it moved outside New York. By spring of 1858, 2,000 met daily in Chicago's Metropolitan Theatre, and in Philadelphia, the meetings mushroomed into a four-month long tent meeting. Meetings were held in Baltimore, Washington, Cincinnati, Chicago, New Orleans, and Mobile. Thousands met to pray because one man stepped out. Annus Mirabilis, the year of national revival, had begun. This was an extraordinary move of God through one man. It was unique because the movement was led by businessmen, a group long considered the least prone to any form of evangelical fervor, and it had started on Wall Street, the most unlikely of all places to begin.

R.G. LeTourneau

R.G. LeTourneau, a businessman from the United States, wrestled with the secular versus full-time Christian work idea. LeTourneau was a successful businessman in the early 1900s that recounts the turning point in his understanding of how God desires to use business for His glory. His pastor one day said to him, "You know, brother LeTourneau, God needs businessmen as well as preachers and missionaries." "Those were the words that guided my life ever since," said LeTourneau. "I repeat them in public at every opportunity because I have discovered that many men have the same mistaken idea I had of what it means to serve the Lord. My idea was if a man was going all out for God, he would have to be a preacher, or evangelist, or a missionary, or what we call a full-time Christian worker. I didn't realize that a layman could serve the Lord as well as a preacher. I left the parsonage in sort of a daze. If God needed businessmen, he could certainly find a lot better material than a dirt-mover with a lot of debts piled up in the garage business. But I said, 'All right, if that is what God wants me to be, I'll try to be His businessman.'" LeTourneau later became known for his generosity for giving 90% of his income to Christian causes.[27]

J.C. Penney

J.C. Penney's name was synonymous with "department store". "He first launched his chain of 'The Golden Rule' stores in 1907. His life was paved

---

[27] R.G. LeTourneau, *Mover of Men and Mountains* (Chicago: Moody Press, 1992), 109-110.

with much adversity throughout his long business career. In 1910 his first wife died. Three years later he incorporated as the J.C. Penney Company. In 1923, his second wife died while giving birth to his son. In 1929, the stock market crashed and he lost $40 million. By 1932, he had to sell out to satisfy creditors. This left Penney virtually broke. Crushed in spirit from his loss and his sudden failing health, Penney wound up in a Battle Creek, Michigan sanitarium. One morning he heard the distant singing of employees who had gathered to start the day with God: "Be not dismayed, whate'er betide, God will take care of you." Penney followed the music to its source and slipped into a back row. He left a short time later a changed man, his health and spirit renewed. Ready at age fifty-six to start the long climb back. By 1951, there was a J.C. Penney store in every state, and for the first time sales surpassed $1 billion a year. The marketplace is where many a person has first found a relationship with God. Penney was known throughout his life for his continued support of Christian charities."[28]

Samuel Morse

Samuel Morse was born in 1791 and grew up desiring to be an artist, and he eventually became very talented and internationally known. However, it was difficult to make a living as an artist in America during that time. A series of crises further complicated his vocational desire when his wife died; then his mother and father also died soon after. He went to Europe to paint and reflect on his life. On his return trip aboard a ship, he was captivated by discussions at dinner about new experiments in electromagnetism. During that important occasion, Morse made the following comment, "If the presence of electricity can be made visible in any part of the circuit, I see no reason why intelligence may not be transmitted by electricity." In the face of many difficulties and disappointments, he determinedly perfected a new invention, and, in 1837, applied for a patent that became what we know today as the telegraph. He also created Morse code. It was only later, after many more setbacks and disappointments, that his projects received funding.

Samuel Morse later commented, "The only gleam of hope, and I cannot underrate it, is from confidence in God. When I look upward it calms any

---

[28] John Woodbridge, *More Than Conquerors*, Moody Press 1992. p.343, Chicago, IL

apprehension for the future, and I seem to hear a voice saying: 'If I clothe the lilies of the field, shall I not also clothe you?' Here is my strong confidence, and I will wait patiently for the direction of Providence." Morse went on to create several other inventions and can be recognized today as the father of faxes, modems, e-mail, the internet and other electronic communication.[29]

A Builder Impacts the Nation of China

Today, God is using men and women in the workplace to impact nations. Space does not permit me to recount the number of modern-day examples of men and women who are impacting their world through Christ. However, I would like to make mention of one man who has become a good friend to Angie and I.

Dale Neill is a commercial builder in Southern California whose business has expanded to the international level. Several years ago Dale went through some major business problems and lost millions of dollars in the process. God saw him through the adversity, and Dale became fully committed to the Lord's purposes in his life because of the things God did during this time. God began to show Dale how He wanted to use business to impact the lives of others.

Dale is now President of the International Christian Chamber of Commerce (ICCC) - USA, and the International Vice President of ICCC. A few years ago a door was opened that allowed a video training course to be developed for the nation of China entitled "You Can Start A Business". China selected ICCC over Microsoft and IBM for this project because they wanted ethics to be presented in the series. This happened because of some ground-work of prayer that had been laid in the nation of China through the leader-ship of ICCC.

Dale and Laurence Holt, another businessman with ICCC from England, were selected by ICCC to head up the video project. Most people said the project would never get off the ground and would end up getting diluted through the political system. Most said it would never air on China TV. Even though ICCC had no background in video training and production, China asked ICCC to do the project. ICCC reminded the government that they were a Christian organization and anything they would teach would be based upon Biblical principles. The Chinese response was that it would be OK, they just could not mention the name of Jesus or say it came from the Bible. ICCC responded by asking, "May we say it is written?" China agreed to allow the statement. That was the door they needed to proceed with the project. The entire series quotes scripture throughout as the basis for the business principles being taught. The series has aired several times on the second largest television network in China with a potential viewing audience of more than 240 million people. The Chinese government has asked ICCC to expand the series significantly and has even given permission to begin the ICCC in the nation.

God is using businessmen and women to take the gospel to un-reached people groups through business. It has been through much sacrificial prayer, giving of resources and time by men and women in the marketplace that this project has moved from birth to its present state of effectiveness. The series is currently being translated into a number of other languages and will be utilized in many countries worldwide, including the inner city of the U.S.

God is looking for men and women who will allow their "staffs" and "donkeys" to be used to perform miracles. Will you allow Him to use yours?

Reflection

1. What is a common theme among those God used to impact their culture?

2. What is required for God to use you to impact your culture?

3. What skill has God given you that He might use in the lives of others?

9

Circumcision in Business

At a lodging place on the way, the LORD met [Moses] and was about to kill him. But Zipporah took a flint knife, cut off her son's foreskin and touched [Moses'] feet with it. "Surely you are a bridegroom of blood to me," she said. So the LORD let him alone. (Ex 4:24-26).

Imagine for a moment that God has spent 80 years preparing Moses to be the man that will free the people of Israel from Egyptian slavery. He spent 40 years of preparation in the court of Pharaoh. He was one of the most educated and cultured persons of his time. As he got older and saw the oppression of his people, he decided to do something about it. Many scholars feel that Moses knew that he was called to free his people. However, Moses made the mistake of trying to free his people in his flesh, so God placed him in the desert for 40 years. The word desert is derived from the Hebrew word *midbaar,* which comes from the word *dahbaar,* meaning, "to speak." God placed Moses in the desert to work out some serious character flaws, and he became the one thing the Egyptians hated the most, a shepherd. It was here in the desert that God spoke to Moses.

When the time came for God to speak to Moses, it came through a burning bush experience. God told him that he was going to send Moses to free the people of Israel and that his staff was a symbol of what was going to be used to demonstrate God's power. We have already stated that the staff represented his occupation as a shepherd.

Now we see Moses ready to fulfill the calling upon his life. He would enter into an intimacy with God that no one on earth had ever had before. The Bible says that God spoke to Moses face-to-face. Now Moses is on his way to Egypt and a strange thing happens. He almost loses his life. And the killer is God Himself because Moses has forgotten to take care of a little detail called "circumcision." Centuries earlier God established a covenant between Abraham and Himself that was signified by circumcision of all male babies. It was to be a sign of the removal of the flesh between God and man. It was painful, bloody and very personal. It was so important to God that He was going to kill Moses, even though God had invested 80 years in preparing this man for this mission. Imagine that! God obviously saw that Moses' oversight was a major blunder that could keep him from receiving the inheritance God had for him. Moses is saved by His wife, and like so many of us men who can't see the forest for the trees, our wives must help us see what we cannot see sometimes.

It is this removal of flesh that is required before God can use a man or woman to become intimate with God and see fruit from this relationship that impacts the Kingdom of God.

Four Stages to Christian Maturity

I have had the privilege to work with men and women in the marketplace movement for several years. Over these years, I have noticed a pattern of spiritual progress among individuals that is consistent with the way God has worked with his leaders in the Bible. These four distinct stages are the 1) Evangelism Stage, 2) Equipping Stage, 3) Empowering Stage, and 4) Engaging Stage. Let me briefly explain each stage.

Evangelism Stage

The Evangelism Stage is the first step in all of our pilgrimages. We meet Christ personally. Our lives are changed. A new birth has occurred. When Jesus called the disciples, all of them were active in their place of work. Peter was fishing. Matthew was collecting taxes. Luke was a physician. At some point, each of them met and began to follow Jesus. This is the first stage of any walk with God. It is the "introduction" stage to a relationship with Jesus.

Equipping Stage

The next stage is the Equipping Stage. This is the time when the believer is discipled and equipped through Bible studies, local church attendance and personal Bible study. During this stage, the individual grows in understanding of the ways of God and knowledge about God. The disciples were personally discipled by Jesus himself. They learned more by what he *did* than through just his words spoken. Throughout the gospels we see where Jesus taught them some principle, but they failed to fully grasp the concept. Jesus seemed to be amused at times of their lack of insight into the principle He was teaching them. They did not fully understand the mission and purpose of the Savior at the time. It was a time of learning about Jesus, but not necessarily knowing Jesus on a deep, intimate level. They lived with Him and watched Him. They tried to model what Jesus taught, but so often they messed things up when they tried things on their own. They did not grasp what it meant to bring the Kingdom of God to the people as Jesus did when He multiplied the five loaves and two fish to feed the 5,000. The disciples were prepared to send the people away. Jesus knew there was a better way. This stage could be further classified as the "knowledge" stage in which we learn a lot about Jesus, but fail to fully understand or experience the power of God in our own lives.

The problem today is that many never advance beyond the Equipping Stage. Earlier we discussed how the Hebrews learned wisdom through obedience while the Greeks learned wisdom through reason and analysis. If we don't move from the head to the heart, we remain in the Equipping Stage.

Empowering Stage

The Empowering Stage is the point of decision for the Christian. It is this stage that I believe is the missing ingredient as to why so many are not living powerful lives that impact the culture where we live. In the Empowering Stage, a person is forced to go outside his own strength and rely on Christ as never before. It is the circumcision of the heart for every person. Many people come into this Empowering Stage as a result of some personal crisis - a business failure, a marriage crisis, a death of a loved one - any number of events can bring the individual to the "end of self." That is precisely the point God wants to make with each of his children - there must be an end to self. God wants a death to take place in every individual. *I have been crucified with Christ and I no longer live, but Christ lives in me. The life I live in the body, I live by the faith in the Son of God, who loved me and gave himself for me* (Galatians 2:20). If we do not pass through this stage, we end up doing lots of things in the flesh like Moses did when he tried to free his people by killing the Egyptian man -- right idea, wrong strategy. Most of us in business must go through a very painful time of learning that we cannot solve every problem ourselves and that our way is NOT always the best way. The pride of life and the power associated with making money is a major vice that Satan uses to keep marketplace people from receiving their full inheritance. It is often the crisis that leads us to the bottom, but it also becomes the catalyst to lead us to a deeper understanding of the ways of God.

Peter is a good example. He met Jesus and walked with Him for three years. He learned everything he could. He kept doing stupid things, but all for the right reason - to please Jesus. He had a lot of raw enthusiasm for God, just like many of us have enthusiasm for God, but until it was tempered through brokenness that leads to total trust, his works resulted in soulish, fleshly acts. It was after Peter denied Jesus three times and fell to his knees in sorrow and repentance that he came to grips with his humanity and the need for Christ. This became the turning point for Peter. It was a necessary step for him to come into the empowering relationship with Jesus and the Holy Spirit.

The church has often prevented this stage from taking place. They have failed to understand its importance. We have been guilty of rescuing too many and shaming those who go through it, somehow associating worldly failure with spiritual failure. When a person enters this circumcision process, we often want to free them from crisis under the guise of Christian mercy. Don't get me wrong; we do need to respond to difficult things people go through, but we must not be too quick to solve every problem. This is not what is needed.

Gunnar Olson once said to me, "It was all I could do not to cut open the cocoon and let you fly out. However, I knew that if I did I would be a hindrance to allowing you to become the man God wanted you to be." At the time, these words were not comforting, but today I am glad he withheld his physical assistance. I was a Christian businessman for twenty years before God allowed me to receive a circumcision of the heart that allowed me to experience Christ fully. That is the purpose for the death experience -- to experience new life, and to experience it more abundantly.

The Empowering Stage is the missing ingredient for many Christians today, especially in the marketplace. This is why we do not see Christians impacting our culture. When a Christian businessperson successfully passes through this Empowering Stage, he becomes a powerful force in the Kingdom of God. R.G. LeTourneau cites this time as the turning point in his life with God. J.C. Penney had a similar encounter that changed his life in his fifties after he had lost everything in the great stock market crash. The men and women who are impacting the Kingdom of God today through business have all gone through an Empowering Stage. It is the "right of passage".

Gunnar Olson is a modern day example of a man who is impacting the Kingdom of God through business. I have shared a little about Gunnar and how he has impacted my life. He is the founder of the International Christian Chamber of Commerce, now operating in over 80 countries. Several years ago God spoke to Gunnar and told him to give all of his money away to a needy family. He was alarmed. When he shared it with his wife they questioned whether this was God. They fasted and prayed and believed it was God. He had been saving to purchase a business and he had two small children at home at the time. Once he determined this was God speaking, he was obedient, giving every cent to the needy family. He had nothing left in savings, in his checking account, or even in his pocket. He did not know where the next meal would come from. He told no one outside his family. This was Gunnar's own "Abraham-Isaac" experience. What you don't know is that Gunnar had been asking God to demonstrate his faithfulness as a provider outside the realm of business. This became how God showed him.

It was a tremendous test that became the central point of Gunnar's relationship with God. Gunnar learned that God could be faithful because he saw firsthand how God miraculously provided for him and his family. Some time later God *gave* Gunnar a business.

Often the Empowerment Stage is signified as a time of real adversity and brokenness. Hebrew 5:8 says that Jesus learned obedience from the things He suffered. Now, I don't know about you, but I never realized that Jesus had to learn obedience. However, suffering is what taught Him obedience. If that is the way He learned obedience, how do you think we are going to learn obedience? So many preachers and marketplace "self-help, positive thinkers" want to associate blessing from God with financial blessing. I believe God wants to bless His children, but there is one thing more important than financial blessing - that is for us to become more Christlike, and to become Christlike means our obedience quotient must continue to rise. In order for the Father to accomplish this in us, it will often mean the removal of some things that hinder this growth.

Another factor in this process is that God teaches us over a lifetime of knowledge and experience. As Christians, we are continually taught the scriptures and encouraged to grow in our knowledge and grace. There comes a point though when our Bible knowledge is tested to let us see whether it has become a part of our life in the way we live. Someone once said that we are never to doubt in darkness what God has shown us in the light. Many times God allows us to walk through the darkness in order to test what we gained in the light. That is how the knowledge becomes fruit.

The Engagement Stage

The Engagement Stage is the last stage. It is the stage when faith becomes works. So often stage one and two are the only stages that many ever achieve. However, those who have successfully gone through the first three stages are motivated to impact their world out of a genuine love of God, not guilt or shame. Their works become an outflow of a life lived in obedience and fellowship with Christ.

Gunnar Olson has impacted nations because of the fruit from his life. R.G. LeTourneau has impacted Christian causes greatly from his giving. (It was said he gave 90% of his income away toward the end of his life). Today, we live in a culture that encourages the Engagement Stage without ever passing through the Empowering Stage. This Engagement Stage can often result in a work of the flesh. You see, many good people want to do good works based on their belief in God. God wants God-things, not good-things. However, unless someone has gone through an Empowering Stage, they may be responding out of guilt and shame. This becomes a sad commentary. Business people begin to use their fleshly business skills to make a spiritual impact, and it doesn't work. This often creates more harm than good.

At the time of Christ the world population on earth was estimated to be around 300 million. There were approximately 5,000 who believed in Jesus during the time He walked on earth. Of those 5,000 it is estimated that 500 actually followed Jesus from place to place and put into practice what Jesus was teaching. However, there were only 12 who lived the life Jesus lived, who died like Jesus died, who identified completely with Christ in all aspects of his life. They had an ongoing, daily relationship with the Savior. Jesus is asking us to have that same kind of relationship with him.

Where does this leave us? If you are a businessperson who desires to follow God, you need to make sure you have had an Empowering Stage in your Christian experience. It does not always mean you must have a crisis in your life. It does mean you must have a death, a circumcision of heart that changes your focus from you, to others -- from self, to Christ. Only Christ can really bring about an Empowering Stage. When it happens, you will be free, and you will see spiritual fruit like never before.

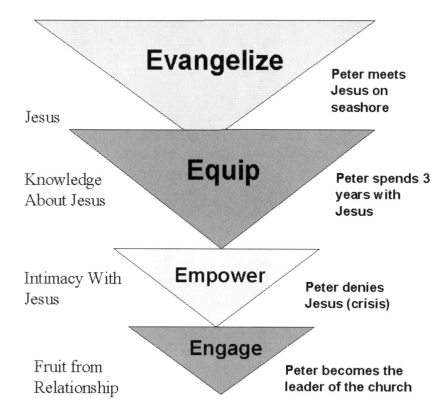

4 Stages of Maturity

Evangelize

Jesus

Peter meets Jesus on seashore

Knowledge About Jesus

Equip

Peter spends 3 years with Jesus

Intimacy With Jesus

Empower

Peter denies Jesus (crisis)

Fruit from Relationship

Engage

Peter becomes the leader of the church

Gospel of the Kingdom Manifested in Workplace

Reflections

1. Based on the four stages presented here, which stage best represents your life at the current time?

2. Have you ever experienced the Crisis Stage? Explain.

3. Why do you think the Empowering Stage is important?

10

3 Attributes of A Modern-Day Kingdom Business

Earlier I mentioned that I believe there is a remnant of men and women God is calling forth to understand their calling and purpose in the workplace. It is a global movement. Over the last few years of this movement, I have noticed three key attributes of this remnant of men and women in the workplace. These attributes appear to be consistent whenever I see the fruit from their life that is impacting the culture and, in many cases, even the nations.

1. Stewardship

"The Lord will make you the head, not the tail. If you pay attention to the commands of the Lord your God that I give you this day and carefully follow then, you will always be at the top, never at the bottom" (Dt. 28:13).

The Lord is raising up a new type of business person that understands stewardship. I believe we are seeing a time in which God is raising up modern-day Josephs who are now coming into the fruitful time of their calling in which they will be entrusted with wealth that will be used to finance the end-time harvest of souls. It will be a time when we finally begin to see Christians become the "heads" instead of the "tails." Joseph was the most powerful man in the world during his service to Pharaoh. However, he never considered the riches of Egypt to be his. He always viewed himself as a steward. Our talents, resources and gifts are to be used through the Lord's guidance to impact our world for the Kingdom of God. Stewardship doesn't just relate to finances, but decision-making too. The true sign of a person who understands stewardship is not in how much they give, but it is in how much they keep. They understand that all we have is the Lord's. We must determine how to be worthy stewards of His resources.

This new breed of business persons understands the need to be account-able to others in the way they make decisions to insure they are not deceived by their own heart (Jer. 17:9). Joseph understood the role of authority in his life. We all must come under the authority of Jesus for decisions that relate to our time, talents, and resources (Rom. 13:1).

2. Intercessory prayer

"Epaphras, who is one of you and a servant of Christ Jesus, sends greetings. He is always wrestling in prayer for you, that you may stand firm in all the will of God, mature and fully assured" (Colossians 4:12).

Intercessory prayer is the second attribute of this new breed of business per-son. God began to lead me to those in the body of Christ who are the inter-cessory prayer warriors. They are a unique breed of individual. I came to real-ize that if we are truly in a battle, then we must have those in the body who are front-line scouts that can warn us against impending attacks and mine-fields. Intercessors are those people.

Intercession is not a spiritual gift but a calling for each believer. Some are called to greater degrees of intercession and often appropriate the gift of prophecy at times. I have come to appreciate the specific role of intercessory prayer in the workplace. Gone are the days of prayer only being used in the local church or for crisis needs alone. God calls us to pray about all things. Now, there is nothing that needs prayer more than the marketplace. God is sounding a trumpet to this need for prayer in order to lay the foundation for what He desires to do in the workplace. Even now, more and more grassroots movements are beginning around prayer in the workplace. One such initiative is the Lighthouse Movement (www.lighthousesatwork.org). This is a coalition of more than 80 denominations, 205,000 churches and more than 400 para-church organizations committed to one goal: prayer. This movement initially began as a movement to enlist people to pray for their neighbors. Once some-one begins to *pray* for their neighbor, they are asked to care for them by serv-ing their needs. Finally, they are asked to *share* with them as God opens a door. It is a simple approach to evangelism that is yielding much fruit. It is now becoming an international movement. Now it has expanded its goals to enlist men and women in the workplace to pray for their co-workers and see God move mightily in this mission field.

Intercessory prayer is best characterized as:

1. Intense prayer for others. (Ephesians 6:18; Colossians 4:12).
2. The priestly calling of all believers, (1 Peter 2:5; Exodus 19:6).
3. The Holy Spirit praying in us. (Romans 8:26,27).

As I have begun to implement prayer into my organization, I have found the following process to be the best application of intercessory prayer in an organization. First, God calls each of us to intercession personally. Then, I consult with my wife on key decisions. Finally, I ask my prayer team to pray over specific things and ask for input as they hear from God. We weigh the feedback that comes from our intercessors and make strategic decisions based on what we believe God is saying to us. We do not believe it is the role of intercessors to dictate strategic action. However, in order to confirm directions and be aware of any "spiritual minefields," I have enlisted intercessory prayer partners with whom I share prayer needs. I look to intercessors for confirmation of what I believe God is saying regarding strategies and actions. Intercessors are not seers and should not be viewed as a crystal ball to determine direction. I do not look to them for upfront direction, which might be contrary to where God appears to be leading. It is the leader's responsibility to work with their staff to implement decisions the leader believes God is revealing. These are important principles when incorporating intercession in a business model. Satan desires to get in the mix in any area that does not have proper Biblical foundations. Please keep this in mind.

Many of you reading this right now are having a real problem with the idea of enlisting others to pray for a for-profit business to succeed in selling products and services, instead of souls. The reason you are having a problem is that you, like myself, have been so entrenched in this "secular versus sacred" model for so long, it is difficult to view a business as a ministry. However, God tells us clearly that we are to glorify God in all that we do (see Col. 3:17, 24). Having people pray for us to fulfill our purpose and calling is consistent with the will of God for every individual. Imagine corporations across the world having a Director of Corporate Intercession as a paid position. I am pleased to tell you it is already happening.

Organizational Model Using Intercessory Prayer

| President | Intercessors | Workers |

Most models like the one above do not show the intercessors as the second item in the chain. Most intercession is the last item. They are often there to give a rubber stamp to what the leadership has already decided. In the above model intercessors are seen as vital to the overall direction of where God is leading.

Introduction to an Intercessor

My first encounter with this was when I was going through a major crisis. I was out of town when a major ministry published a story about me. An intercessor named Jan Christie called to learn more about my work. She was surprised to learn I lived in the same area as she, so she came by our office and met with another woman on our staff. After visiting for a little while, Jan asked if we could spend time praying together. She knew little of me or anyone else in my office, yet when she began praying she said she saw a picture of three men and began to describe each one in detail. At the conclusion of her prayer our staff person said, "You just described the three men in our office." That was the beginning of my introduction to an "intercessor." Jan has since become my intercessory prayer director and is now a vital part of the ministry God has called me to in the workplace.

A few years ago, I was on a trip to meet with some partners on a ministry venture. For months I had been troubled about the direction this venture was taking. However, I had not been able to clearly discern whether my issue was "my issue" or something that God wanted addressed. I had not shared this with Jan but had asked her simply to pray about something I was concerned about. The concern had related to a very "foundational issue" within the ministry. The next morning I checked my e-mail and Jan had sent me a note that said she was praying and God seemed to impress her to encourage me to address boldly anything that was on my heart, especially anything that was "foundational." She actually used those words. This was confirmation for me to know that what I was sensing was from God. This gave me boldness to address my concern.

Five Points

The last several years I have come to know some incredible men and women of God. One such friend is Emeka Nwankpa from Nigeria. Emeka has been trained as a barrister in the nation of Nigeria. However, in the last several years God has trained him as an intercessor and he is director of intercession for the International Christian Chamber of Commerce and has directed intercessory prayer for the nation of Nigeria. He shared this amazing story at our second Marketplace Leaders Summit a few years ago.

"I had to handle a case on appeal. In preparing for that case, I had written out a brief for five grounds of appeal. I had prayed. My wife had prayed. My junior in chambers had prayed. That morning I came into court. I tried to talk to some of the senior members of the bar to see if they could give me any tips. Because this legislation was very new at the time, the case law on it was very little. It had not been recorded for people to get out of law reports. So here I am in court and I bow my head and I begin to pray. And the Spirit of God told me, 'Cancel grounds one through four, argue ground five.'

Since it was me who was to start, the judge said, 'Well, proceed.' 'Your Lordship, I first want to inform the court that I wish to withdraw grounds one through four.' He said, 'Counsel, are you sure you want to do this?' 'Yes, your Lordship.' 'Well, grounds one through four are struck out. Proceed on ground five,' said the judge. I finished my argument on ground five and I sat down. The lawyer on the other side got up and for twelve minutes could not get a word out of his mouth! He opened it, closed it, turned this way, then that way, and he stammered; then he finally said, 'It is unfortunate that my learned friend has withdrawn grounds one to four.' He sat down and resigned the case. I found out later he had prepared grounds one to four and had nothing for ground five. So, you know who won the case.

Even in the nitty gritty of daily life the spiritual realm is more real than the physical. The spiritual realm controls the physical. In fact, if you win a battle in the spiritual realm, you can be sure the physical realm will follow suit."

Cautions To Implementing Corporate Intercessory Prayer

There are a few cautions I wish to voice at this point. As mentioned, anything can be knocked off track when we get out of balance. Here are just a few things to keep in mind when starting a intercessory prayer in a business.

1. Avoid moving based on one intercessor's input. Gain agreement through more than one source.
2. Try to have a proper mix of male and female individuals on your intercessory team.
3. You are responsible for the final decision. You should have a peace about this decision but be willing to commit it to the Lord should it not fit your rationale all the time.
4. It does require work and additional time.

Practical Implementation

1. Begin praying for God to identify intercessors.
2. Ask your pastor who the intercessors are in your church that might be willing to be on your team.
3. Develop a few test situations that you run past your intercessors before the decision is made.

Compensation

Obviously associating compensation with intercessory prayer is a very sensitive issue. Some businesses have people who do other jobs in their businesses, but have a real calling to intercession. In this way they are not perceived as being "paid to pray" even though theologically I have no problem with this. However, the potential for abuse in this is great and you should exercise caution in associating money with prayer. There are other ways you might consider compensating those who are committing time to your business besides finances. One of the ways is setting up a foundation that can contribute to an intercession fund that is disbursed to those who might be interceding as part of their primary call in life. A donor directed foundation can be set up for minimal expense.

3. Pioneer Spirit

Joshua Told the people, "Consecrate yourselves, for tomorrow the LORD will do amazing things among you" (Josh. 3:5).

So, when the people broke camp to cross the Jordan, the priests carrying the ark of the covenant went ahead of them. Now the Jordan is at flood stage all during harvest. Yet, as soon as the priests who carried the ark reached the Jordan and their feet touched water's edge, the water from upstream stopped flowing (Josh 3:14-16).

When the people of Israel were about to cross over into the much awaited Promised Land, the priests were instructed to carry the ark of the covenant in front of them. Forty years of wandering in the desert and the time finally arrived. Joshua was told by the Lord that the priests were to carry the ark into the Jordan River, God did not tell Joshua or the people what would happen after that. They simply had to obey the Lord. Now the Jordan River was at flood stage, which meant that the banks were high and the water was flowing at a pretty good pace. Christian archaeologists say that in order to enter the Jordan from the bank at flood stage was a risky proposition. They would have to gently place one foot in front of another and make sure of their footing. I could hear the priests talking just before they were to make this historic crossing. "What if we lose it?! I could never live this down!" On the other hand, God told them to do this so they did have the assurance that if things did not turn out, it would not be their fault. A willingness to take risks and trust God in areas where we cannot see how things are going to turn out is the definition of faith. If we can see the outcome, it is not faith. The Bible says the priests placed their toes into the water and immediately the Jordan backed up and kept the water completely retrained. In fact, the wet riverbed became dry! The priests walked into the reverbed and stood there while the entire nation crossed. Imagine the relief that must have come over these men. What joy they must have felt! God did another miracle and they were able to see it first hand.

A pioneer spirit means having the spirit of Joshua and Caleb who did not see the giants in the land; instead, they saw what God wanted to do. They saw the potential. They saw what God saw. Someone once said, "Attempt something so great for God that it is doomed for failure unless God be in it." I agree with the statement as long as God is the one telling you to attempt it. Too many times we attempt something God never told us to attempt. Then we blame God for the failure. So if God tells you to go for it, GO FOR IT!

I have been excited to meet so many men and women around the world today who have this pioneer spirit. They see with spiritual eyes and take that first step without knowing where it will lead. They are willing to risk their money and time if they believe God is in it.

Did Jesus Have A Pioneer Spirit?

Jesus gave them this answer: "I tell you the truth, the Son can do nothing by Himself; He can do only what He sees His Father doing, because whatever the Father does the Son also does (John 5:19).

Jesus never did anything He didn't see His Father doing. This was His only mode of operation. He didn't do things because He thought it was a good idea. He only did something if it was a God-idea. As an entrepreneur myself the hardest thing I must wrestle with is whether something is a good idea or a God-idea. Good ideas won't have the anointing of God on them; God ideas always have the anointing of God.

I remember when I attempted to launch a workshop called Marketing the Church back in the mid-eighties. I developed a complete workshop with marketing materials and direct mail brochures to mail to churches. The first workshop I taught was a miserable failure. The people were not blessed. They did not feel they gained anything. God's anointing was not on it so it never got past the first few workshops before we decided to can it. Part of the problem was that I didn't understand this spiritual principle like I do today. I compare this to when I began writing daily marketplace meditations for business associates and circulating them via e-mail. It was done out of a heart to minister to others and I had little hopes for anything to come from it. Soon, as I shared these, more and more people requested to be added to my e-mail list. It got to be more than 200 subscribers when a friend and internet website owner suggested that he manage the subscriptions from his website. It then began to grow at more than 500 new subscribers a month. Soon it was added to other websites. The subscription got to 24,000 a day with more than 1,000 being added each month. I began receiving mail from people all over the world because of the impact it was having on them. Now it is distributed around the world and has become a book of 365 marketplace meditations known as *TGIF Today God Is First.* This has opened up an entire ministry for me. It began with an idea. However, I must confess I had to overcome the fear of failure because I knew my grammar was weak and I had no resources to hire someone. I had to decide whether my fear of this (like Moses' fear of speaking) was going to be stronger than my willingness to be a blessing to someone. Strangely enough, God provided an editor just months later in the form of an English teacher working in Japan who was a subscriber and noticed I needed a little help. He edited for me free of charge by exchanging e-mail from Atlanta to Japan. God does things in strange ways that are almost ALWAYS different from the way we would do it. The key to His way is simple faith and simple obedience. That is all that He asks of us. He will do the rest if He is leading us.

Do you have a pioneer spirit? If you don't, ask God to give you a pioneer spirit that is willing to take a faith risk. A friend once said that if God is leading, then it is not a risk. I disagreed with my friend because there was at least a "perceived risk" for the priests when they stepped into that river. However, God was going ahead of them, and I believe that if we make faith decisions from a pure heart motive God will pave the way in front of us.

Reflection

1. How would you describe yourself as a steward of time, talent and resources?

2. How would you describe your level of intercessory prayer?

3. Would others classify you as one having a pioneer spirit? Explain why they would or would not.

11

The Missing Weapon:
Unity in the Army of God

... in Judah the hand of God was on the people to give them <u>unity of mind to carry out what the king and his officials had ordered</u>, following the word of the LORD (2Chr. 30:12 emphasis mine).

The Armed Forces comprise four unique defense services including the Army, Navy, Marines, and Air Force. Each armed service section of the military has a unique role to play in time of national crisis. Each branch of service knows the particular role they are to play in mounting an army that can defend our country. The Air Force would not expect the Army to send air strikes. The Army would not expect the Air Force to provide ground troops. Each one of these has *one mission* - to win the war. They represent *separate callings* - each with a unique role to play, and they are each one part of *many alliances.* When brought together, they are a powerful force. When used alone, they have significantly less power. The body of Christ needs to understand the power of unity.

Perhaps you might think it strange that I would end this book with a chapter on unity. Well, the truth is that you and I cannot be successful in appropriating Christ in the workplace unless we are unified in many different areas. First, we must be unified in our relationship with Jesus. Jesus said that we are to abide in Him like a vine. *I am the vine; you are the branches. If a man remains in me and I in him, he will bear much fruit; apart from me you can do nothing* (John 15:5). There you have it. You can't do anything for the Kingdom unless you are unified with Jesus. Second, you cannot be effective in reaching the marketplace unless there is unity among other Christians, other churches, and other marketplace ministries.

*May they be <u>brought to complete unity to let the world know that You sent Me</u>
and have loved them even as You have loved Me* (John 17:23 emphasis mine).

This passage of scripture has been burning on my heart for the last four years.
I cannot escape the implication; if we want the world to know that God sent
Jesus and we want the world to respond to Him, then we need to become
unified. Jesus is telling us the formula for success --- a unified army. God will
not let us be successful in the things of God until there is unity. It is that simple.

F.B. Meyer saw that his congregation was dwindling from Sunday to
Sunday. One day he asked a close friend and member why he felt the attendance was down. The friend told him of a young preacher who was attracting
many to his church. His name was Charles Spurgeon. F.B. Meyer said, "If that
is the case then I think we should all go down to his church today and see
this move of God. God is obviously moving in this man's life." Now that man
is secure in God! How many preachers do you know willing to do such a
thing? How many ministries do you know that will bless a "competing" ministry?

In the October issue of *Moody Magazine* a statistic was cited that blew my
mind. There are more than 24,000 Christian denominations in the world and
five new ones start every week. David Barrett of the International Bulletin puts
this number at 34,000 in the year 2000. Regardless of which number is more
accurate, how do you think Jesus feels about this? What does this say about
unity in the body of Christ?

However, there are some positive signs on the horizon. God IS unifying
His church. He is breaking down racial walls. He is bringing pastors together
in cities. He is bringing men together to pray and seek God on behalf of their
families to fulfill Godly leadership in their homes. He is raising up reconcilia-
tion ministries designed to break down generational strongholds in countries
and cities. On the other hand, we are a long way from mobilizing the army
that God really wants to mobilize. There is still much work to be done. Why
does God want unity in the body of Christ? It's simple. He cannot return until
people have heard the gospel and they cannot hear the gospel through a frac-
tured church.

Unifying the Army

If you have gotten to this section of the book, you now realize that there is a move of God taking place in the workplace around the world. God is raising up an army in his remnant of the church called the marketplace.

Even the corporate marketplace has learned the benefit of working together. Texaco has learned the benefit of having a Burger King restaurant in their gasoline stations. Wal-Mart has learned there is a benefit to having McDonald's inside their stores. Dunkin' Donuts has learned that they can attract more customers if they have Baskin Robbins inside their stores. The list could go on. The lesson is obvious. There are benefits to partnerships and alliances that allow us to serve more people and achieve greater impact.

However, there is even a greater reason that there should be a more unified church.

> It was he who gave some to be apostles, some to be prophets, some to be evangelists, and some to be pastors and teachers, to prepare God's people for works of service, so that the body of Christ may be built up until we all reach unity in the faith and in the knowledge of the Son of God and become mature, attaining to the whole measure of the fullness of Christ (Eph 4:11-13). And over all these virtues put on love, which binds them all together in perfect unity (Col. 3:14).

God wants us to come to the whole measure of the fullness of Christ, which is only reached by unity in the faith.

What Can Happen When Unity Spreads

The following story was printed in the *1998 Religion Today* news story.

Prayer Unifies Pastors, Cities

Spending hours of unhurried time with God is transforming pastors, their churches, and their communities.

...Four-day retreats called Prayer Summits are "exploding around the world," Terry Dirks told *Religion Today*. He runs the summits as president of international Renewal Ministries, part of Portland, Ore.-based Multnomah Bible College and Biblical Seminary

...Summits are being held in 130 cities and 13 nations this year, Dirks said. Most have been held in the United States, while others have taken place in Japan, Poland, Russia, Israel, Australia, Canada, and Mexico. Most participants are white evangelicals, but more are coming from mainline churches and minority communities, he said. Each summit includes participants from many different churches in the same geographical area.

...The only agenda at the retreats is to seek God. "No church business is allowed. No strategizing or networking," Joe Aldrich, founder of the Prayer Summits, said. "What we need is time in his presence, to worship him hour after hour."

...When pastors spend time "with their common King" they feel safe and leave their differences behind, Aldrich said. They become humble and often are surprised by what they agree on and share.

...Changes remain after the summits conclude. "Denominational barriers that came down stay down," Aldrich said. Relationships develop as pastors hold joint church services and exchange pulpits with their rediscovered brothers -- who once viewed each other quite differently." The pastors "can't return to business as usual."

...Pastors become co-laborers in the gospel those who run the summits say. They pray for and help each other rather than criticize and compete. Churches become unified. "The church becomes a vital, healthy community of faith," Dirks said. It's "the one church in the one body of Christ in that city."

...It is "not unity for unity's sake," Dirks said, "but so that non-Christians will believe that Jesus is who he said he is." Prayer Summits, which started in Portland in 1989, have resulted in nearly 1,000 ongoing pastor's prayer groups.

...After pastors have prayed together for four or five years, they begin to :ask what's next," Dirks said. Leaders who have emerged among the pastors then meet together. International Renewal Ministries helps them to discuss ways to cooperatively evangelize their city or region for Christ. About 20 such consultations have been held in the last few years.

...Other types of retreats have begun as an offshoot of the Prayer Summits. These include retreats tailored for pastor's wives, pastors and their wives, lay leaders, women in leadership positions, youth workers, missions' executives, denominational leaders, church boards, business executives, and college students.

"God is stirring in the hearts of his people, drawing them to him and to one another," Dirks said.[30]

Restoring the Marketplace To God's Economy

> *Then the LORD replied: "Write down the revelation and make it plain on tablets so that a herald may run with it. For the revelation awaits an appointed time; it speaks of the end and will not prove false. Though it linger, wait for it; it will certainly come and will not delay"* (Hab. 2:2-3).

When I first met Jan Christie, my intercessory prayer director, she shared how God had impressed upon her that He wanted to restore the marketplace to God's economy. When I asked her about this she said that it did not necessarily mean a financial economy, but a way of operating in the marketplace that was honoring to God. Imagine what God's economy might look like if He were to totally infiltrate the marketplace with His love and power and grace. Perhaps we might see and hear news headlines like the following;

---

[30] Reprinted by permission, *ReligionToday.com*, March 18, 1999. International Renewal Ministries is at 8435 N.E. Gilsan St., Portland, OR 97220.

Future Headlines?

"Christian CEOs ban together and commit their corporate profits to feeding the poor in India."

"Group of Christian philanthropists and business owners pool $300 million to present claims of Christ on network television."

"Special noon-day prayer meetings held daily in Wal-mart."

"Wall Street executives meet on the floor of the stock exchange to pray for God's blessing on the nation and economy."

"Christian led Congress passes bill to repeal Rowe vs Wade. Supreme court unanimously endorses bill four days later."

"500 executives make decisions for Christ at GM corporate annual meeting."

"CBS features program on how Christianity in the workplace transformed bankrupted Wall Street Investment Company."

"China establishes new government based upon the Bible. Communism a thing of the past."

"Prayer is re-instituted in public schools."

"Churches pool money together to transform downtown slum area. Model city has been created."

"AT&T renounces policies supporting gay rights. Cites Bible as reason for policy change."

Are these headlines far-fetched idealistic dreams? If it had not already taken place, I might agree with you. However, we now know that God can and does transform entire cities when prayer and unity are combined in a city.

Transformations

What I am talking about is not just a metaphorical application of the Scriptures, but what takes place when a marketplace Christian has a genuine encounter and transformation that results in a life that impacts the culture. When this takes place, we see how a community, a city, and a nation is restored to God's economy through marketplace Christians. This is the difference between the Gospel of Salvation - focused mainly on salvation—and the Gospel of the Kingdom—where the gospel is impacting and transforming the culture. The following diagram illustrates this principle.

This diagram represents three stages of growth towards obedience and love for Jesus Christ. As the person flows, progressively from the top to the bottom, a greater degree of love and obedience takes place. At the bottom of the funnel is the place where a Christian begins to live a victorious Christian life that yields much fruit. This is the place where the Gospel of the Kingdom is manifested, not just the Gospel of Salvation.

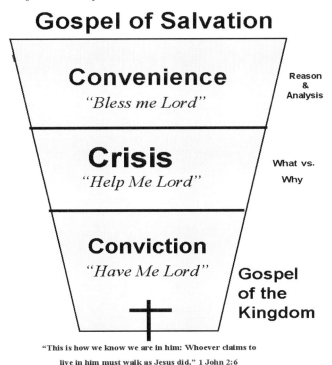

Gospel of Salvation

Convenience
"Bless me Lord"

Reason & Analysis

Crisis
"Help Me Lord"

What vs. Why

Conviction
"Have Me Lord"

Gospel of the Kingdom

"This is how we know we are in him: Whoever claims to live in him must walk as Jesus did." 1 John 2:6

Convenience Gospel

The top of the diagram represents the widest opening, the place where most Christians enter through the grace of Christ. It is a free gift. Sometimes salvation comes because it is simply a good proposition - eternal life is gained simply for asking and repenting. Many Christians remain in the upper part of this diagram. They are satisfied to be saved, but their life does not go much deeper spiritually. Thus, they do not impact the culture. This is best signified by a "Bless me Lord" attitude.

Crisis

The second phase of this diagram signifies those Christians who either enter the Kingdom of God through a crisis, or they are Christians who enter a crisis time in their lives. We have all heard of "foxhole Christians." There is a place of obedience for all of us in order to get out of our pain. In this place we seek God for the "What" or "Why" answers. We want to know what or why we are experiencing difficulty in our lives so that we can fix it. This is signified by a "Help Me Lord" attitude.

Conviction

The final stage is the conviction stage. It is the place where the Christian is motivated out of love for the Savior. This person does not need a benefit to seek God nor is he seeking God for His hand. He is seeking in order to know the Savior more intimately. It is here that intimacy with God yields fruit that impacts communities, cultures and nations. It is here that the person understands why Jesus said, *"This is how we know we are in him: Whoever claims to live in him must walk as Jesus did"* (1 John 2:6).

Almolonga, Guatemala

Almolonga is a town of only 20,000 people in Guatemala. Twenty years ago, this city was one of the worst cities in the nation. The poverty, violence and spirit worship resulted in a people and community that were spiritually and physically bankrupt. There were four jails in the city and alcohol and drug abuse were rampant. The community lived in a farming area that depended upon produce sales for their primary source of income. During this period, the land was so arid that it yielded only four truck loads of produce a month.

There was a pastor in that city that began to pray. He began to fast with other intercessors three or four times a week. Over a period of time people began to get saved. Lives began to change. The intercessors prayed against the spirit worship that had so impacted this city. As more and more people became changed by the power of the gospel, the city began to plant seeds of new life. The negative influences began to be overcome. Miracle stories of healings and other extraordinary happenings were reported. People were interested to know more because of the change they saw in their friends.

Now, twenty years later, the community of Almolonga is a transformed model city. Pastors and other Christian leaders pray together and fast three or four times a week, and 80% of the town are born again Christians. The jail has now closed due to the lack of crime in the city. There are now two dozen evangelical churches in the city and God is even touching the agricultural community in a very unusual and miraculous way. As mentioned, they were only delivering four truckloads of produce a month. Now, they are delivering forty truckloads a week --- a 1000% increase! However, that is not the most remarkable thing. The produce they are harvesting is many times larger than the size of normal produce. Beets are 4 pounds, lettuce is the size of basketballs, and carrots are the size of a man's arm. If I had not seen it on video with my own eyes, I would not have believed it! Farmers pay cash for Mercedes trucks and place Christian names on their trucks. This community is sold out for Christ, and Christ seems to be sold out for them in every way. This is what I mean by the Kingdom of God being manifested in a physical way.

This is not the only community that has experienced such a transformation by God. The Sentinel Group, a ministry in Lynnwood, Washington has done a one-hour video documentary on four different communities, one of which is Almolonga. However, the good news is there are more and more cities being transformed around the world.

The question for you and me is, "How can God use men and women in the marketplace like yourself to impact communities, cities, and even nations?" I hope I have been successful in explaining what I believe is necessary for this to happen. Let me assure you, God wants to demonstrate His love and power through your vocation, no matter how menial or unimportant you may feel it is.

Now, may God grant you the same request that the mother of Jabez prayed for her son.

> *Now Jabez was more honorable than his brothers, and his mother called his name Jabez, saying, "Because I bore him in pain." And Jabez called on the God of Israel saying, "Oh, that You would bless me indeed, and enlarge my territory, that Your hand would be with me, and that You would keep me from evil, that I may not cause pain!" So, God granted him what he requested* (1 Chron 4:9-10 NKJ).

Yes, Lord. may you enlarge our territory for your name's sake. Amen.

Reflections

1. What stage in life do you see yourself: convenience, crisis, or convictions?

2. What would restoring the Marketplace to God's economy look like at your workplace?

3. Why is unity key to the world seeing Christ manifested? What can you do to increase unity in your sphere of influence?

Faith & Work WebSites

Following is a partial listing of website addresses for ministries that serve the workplace. For a complete listing go to www.marketplaceleaders.org, www.scruples.org, www.lighthousesatwork.org, or www.wowi.net (FaithAtWork Directory).

www.markeplaceleaders. org Marketplace Leaders
www.lighthousesatwork.org Lighthouses at Work
www.wowi.net Workplace Wisdom Interactive
www.iccc.net International Christian Chamber of Commerce
www.lifeatwork.com Life@Work magazine
www.faithworks.org Faith Works Ministries
www.scruples.org YWAM Marketplace Ministries
www.aclj.org American Center for Law and Justice
www.fcci.org Fellowship of Companies for Christ International
www.cbmc.com CBMC
www.sf.org/c/cnt Christian Network Team
www.cbmcint.org International Division of CBMC
www.avodaInstitue.org Avodah Institute
www.marketplaceministries.com Marketplace Ministries
www.ibelieve.com iBelieve.com
www.lovingmonday.com Loving Monday
www.cmdsemas.ca Christian Medical and Dental Society
www.cibn.net Christian International Business Network
www.iccc-usa.net International Christian Chamber of Commerce - USA
www.Godisworking.com ROI Ministries
www.tentmaking.org Canadian Tentmaker Network
www.fgbmfi.org Full Gospel Businessmen's Fellowship International
www.icba.com International Christian Business Association
www.bpn.org Business and Professional Network
www.needleseye.org Needles Eye Ministries
www.cedarville.edu Journal of Biblical Integration
www.christianworkingwoman.org Christian Working Woman
www.gostrategic.org Strategic Christian Services
www.probe.org Probe Ministries
www.meda.org Mennonite Economic Development Association
www.lifepurpose.org Life Purpose Ministries
www.la-red.org laRed Business Network

Faith & Work WebSites - Con't.

www.faithatwork.org Faith@Work Ministries
www.christiansincommerce.org Christians in Commerce
www.ybl.org Young Business Leaders
www.priorityasscociates.org Priority Associates
www.jesusceo.com Jesus CEO
www.ministrydg.com Ministry Development Group
www.fcci.org Fellowship of Companies for Christ
www.willowcreek.org Executive Women's Ministry
www.gospelcom.net/iv/md/aboutmdl/ Ministry in Daily Life
www.bpnavigators.org Business & Professional Ministry
www.thec12group.com C12 Groups
www.businessproverbs.org Business Proverbs
www.ifcb.org International Fellowship of Christian Businessmen

Marketplace Leaders

Marketplace Leader's purpose is to raise up and train men and women to fulfill their calling in and through the workplace and to view their work as their ministry.

Our primary means of accomplishing this is through four key focuses.

1. Building Unity (John 17:23) –
Marketplace Leader Summits are held to encourage unity among marketplace ministries serving men and women in the workplace. See www.icwm.net.

Our *TGIF Monthly* is a monthly e-mail bulletin for marketplace ministries to inform and communicate the various services and activities of marketplace ministries. Our website also features many articles and resources.

2. Training New Leaders
Our workshops are designed to raise up and encourage men and women through mentoring and training programs.

Called to the Workplace–From Esau to Joseph one-day workshops are designed to help Christians understand their calling in the workplace.

TGIF Today God Is First marketplace meditations is a free daily e-mail devotional that encourages you to put God first in the workplace. It is distributed via the internet to thousands daily around the world. (visit our website to subscribe.)

Marketplace Mentor is a monthly teaching newsletter that features indepth articles on faith and work distributed by e-mail.

3. Publishing
Marketplace Leaders develops new resources targeted for Christians in business including *Called to the Workplace – Esau to Joseph* audio tape/workbook and an *Online Catalog* of resources specifically selected for workplace Christians.

4. Consulting
Marketplace Leaders provides marketing consulting to organizations to help them in the development of their companies from a Biblical perspective. Strategic planning, marketing, and creative communications are services we provide.

Let us know how we can assist you in furthering your organization. Call Os Hillman at 678-455-6262 or contact him via e-mail at os@marketplaceleaders.org.

Marketplace Leaders
Telephone: 678-455-6262
Fax: 678-455-6264

E-mail: os@marketplaceleaders.org
Web site: www.marketplaceleaders.org

Other Resources by Os Hillman

TGIF Today God Is First
365 Meditations on the Principles of Christ in the Workplace.
hardback
It began as a series of daily e-mail meditations for his business associates. Today, it is one of the fastest growing devotionals on the internet and is now a book of 365 daily meditations especially geared for men and women in the workplace. Os has the uncanny ability to write just to people's circumstances to help men and women understand how to walk with God in the everyday trials of life.

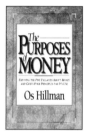

The Purposes of Money
Exposing Five Fallacies and God's Design in Financial Blessing
softcover
One day a series of crises entered the world of this successful advertising agency executive that would alter his life forever. These life-changing events led him to discover wrong priorities and how many business people have erroneously viewed money. Questions for reflection at the end of each section make this 80-page book excellent for individual and group study.

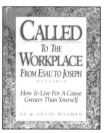

Called to the Workplace: From Esau to Joseph
How To Live For A Cause Greater Than Yourself
audio tape series, $95.00
Called to the Workplace: From Esau to Joseph is a six-tape audio series with workbook that is Os Hillman's complete one-day workshop. This workshop helps men and women discover their purpose in work and life. This workshop is loaded with practical application principles to understand God's method of calling, Biblical decision-making, and the role adversity plays in every believers life. *(Not available in stores. See our website to order.*

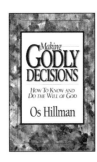

Making Godly Decisions
How To Know and Do the Will of God

softcover

In *Making Godly Decisions,* Os Hillman provides a thorough look, through scripture and personal experience, at principles for making good decisions. Hillman provides real-life case studies from others and from his own spiritual journey that will show you how to apply these principles.

Adversity & Pain: The Gifts Nobody Wants
Discover God's Purposes for Adversity in Our Lives.

softcover

"Hillman's vulnerability in relating his own suffering adds a personal and compassionate tone to a thorough presentation of the purpose and usefulness of pain in Christians' lives. Hillman's recurring theme is that God is GOD, and His reign over our lives isn't intended to be a democracy."

–Kris Wilson, March 1997 *CBA Marketplace Magazine Review*

TGIF Bible Study
Small Group Bible Study Book

softcover

The popular TGIF, Today God Is First book is now a 12-week, small group Bible study book. It is based on 12 devotionals pertaining to your Calling in the workplace. The book is ideal for workplace groups that are just getting started, or for facilitators who want to try something new.

Marketplace Leaders
3520 Habersham Club Dr. Cumming, GA 30041 USA
Telephone: 678-455-6262 Fax: 678-455-6264
www.marketplaceleaders.org

NOTES:

NOTES:

NOTES:

NOTES:

NOTES:

NOTES:

NOTES:

NOTES:

NOTES:

NOTES:

NOTES:

NOTES:

NOTES:

NOTES:

NOTES: